TELEVISION AND THE CLASSROOM

Don Kaplan

Knowledge Industry Publications, Inc.
White Plains, NY and London

Video Bookshelf

Television and the Classroom

Library of Congress Cataloging-in-Publication Data

Kaplan, Don.
    Television and the classroom.

    (Video bookshelf)
    Bibliography: p.
    Includes index.
    1. Television in education—United States.
2. Television—United States—Psychological aspects.
I. Title.   II. Series.
LB1044.7.K318   1986   371.3'3584   86-7321
ISBN 0-86729-138-9 (pbk.)

Printed in the United States of America

10   9   8   7   6   5   4   3   2   1

Contents

List of Tables and Figures

List of Photos

Introduction

Television has been blamed for everything from declining SAT scores to increasing violence among the young; from provoking riots to creating "vidiots." Opponents say TV shortens attention spans, decreases the ability to process written information, inhibits creativity and original thinking, and interferes with socialization and the general learning process. Some proponents claim that TV provides a window on the world that exposes viewers to events and places they might not otherwise see, while others say that it gives the public exactly what it wants: programs that merely entertain and have no further social impact.

For most Americans, television serves as a primary source of entertainment and information. For youngsters especially, it may often replace the family, the school and real life experiences as the major socializing institution. According to Marieli Rowe, executive director of the National Telemedia Council:

> Television and the media-dominated society in which we live, have created a new environment and a new dimension in our children's growth. This 'media information society' floods our daily lives and alters dramatically a child's natural progression of life experiences. Where previously, his growing years followed a normal sequence of expanding horizons, from home and neighborhood to school and community, and finally, after some years, to the greater world outside, television has changed all this. Demands on the child's judgment are greater and they come earlier.[1]

The statistics are all too familiar: by the age of 18, the average American child has watched over 22,000 hours of TV—more hours in front of a TV set than inside a classroom.[2] And although youngsters aren't actively pursuing knowledge when they watch TV, that doesn't mean they aren't learning or absorbing something. During all

1

those hours of viewing, children may be learning that happiness and satisfaction are measured by what and how much they buy. They may be absorbing misconceptions such as the idea that conflicts are best resolved by force and violence or that complex problems can be solved in five minutes (or even more quickly by taking a pill), or that successful people are attractive and wealthy, or that cosmetics and detergents can conceal or wash away their problems. Many critics believe that TV influences the decisions children make about sexuality, health, personal relations and careers, and that it gives them unrealistic notions of what they can expect from adults.

As Rosemary Lee Potter points out in *New Season* (one of the few books that focus on the positive uses of television), TV is one of the most pervasive forces in children's lives.[3] In *The Plug-In Drug,* Marie Winn goes even further by describing TV as *the* most important influence in children's lives today.[4] Numerous studies (noted in the following pages) have demonstrated the influence TV has on children's attitudes about themselves, others and the world. If you have any doubts about children's abilities to learn behavioral patterns from TV, just ask your students to mimic the actions and speech patterns of their favorite TV characters.

Despite the impact TV has on youngsters, teachers are often reluctant to use television in the classroom. They may feel that students are already spending too much time watching television programs and consider TV to be too contemporary or faddish to be taken seriously (especially when students are having difficulty with reading and writing). There are other childhood interests that could be and are explored in class—but none that is so present in most children's daily lives, occupies such a large amount of their time, is shared to such a large degree by their peers, maintains their interest on an ongoing basis, or is as readily accessible.

When integrated with the curriculum, TV can become an additional resource to help teachers make better use of classroom time. Focused viewing assignments that ask students to be accountable for what they are viewing can become a part of the regular course of study. These assignments can be used to help students develop basic skills such as the ability to identify main ideas, separate fact from fiction and understand plot structure.

By providing opportunities for students to talk about TV, educators can turn passive viewing (the major criticism directed against television) into active learning and reinforce rather than take time away from other subject areas. Discussion about specific programs is one of the best ways to help students deal with television and combat its negative effects. While other media events become special occasions that are anticipated, discussed and evaluated, much of what is seen by children on television is absorbed passively without interpretation.

Television and the Classroom is intended to help educators look at commercial TV not as an adversary but as a learning tool—one that can have positive educational value and one that (not so incidentally) appeals to students. The questions for discussion, activities and background materials provided here can enable students to examine some of television's many aspects. Suggested assignments may also help students to better understand the effects TV has on them and can aid them in making informed viewing decisions. By answering questions such as "Why do you watch TV?" and "What do you enjoy or dislike about the programs you watch?" students can begin to think about television as more than just a time killer. They can develop critical viewing skills and demand more from the programs they watch.

By participating in these discussions and activities, students can also learn to:

- question the behaviors and "realities" they see acted out on TV
- question generalizations they make based on stereotypes they see on TV
- explore alternatives to violence as solutions to problems
- examine the business of TV and how it affects schedules, informational programming and program content
- identify persuasive techniques that can be used to manipulate viewers
- clarify their own values and taste as opposed to those shown on TV

By using what students are already watching as a starting point, teachers can introduce background material and activities into the classroom to help students explore a variety of topics.

It can be helpful to assign specific TV programs for viewing by students. If students are familiar with the characters and general plots of the programs assigned, discussion may also flow more easily. Networks often provide guides to specials and miniseries that can provide information weeks in advance of the air date of some broadcasts. It should be kept in mind that when examining shows, programs should not be limited to those made especially for children or programs broadcast during the "family hour." Eighty percent of the time, children are watching programs made for adults. Statistics show that 11 million children below the age of 12 are still watching TV between the hours of 9:00 p.m. and 9:30 p.m., 9.7 million are watching between 9:30 p.m. and 10:00 p.m., 6.8 million between 10:00 p.m. and 10:30 p.m., 5.6 million between 10.30 p.m. and 11:00 p.m. and over a million young children are still watching TV at midnight.[5]

References in the text to specific programs have been avoided. Activities can therefore be used with programs of any season and can be modified for different age groups and/or levels of sophistication. (Although activities aren't divided by age level, there are general activities for younger students and more complex assignments for older students.)

The activities suggested may not compensate for the types of learning that would be taking place if your students weren't watching television, but they can help you to take the best advantage of that time to foster every child's learning.

NOTES

1. Marieli Rowe, "Media Literacy: The New Challenge," *Better Broadcast News* 27 (March-April 1981): 1, 6.

2. "Family Learning Guide," *Family Learning* (May/June 1984): 2, 7.

3. Rosemary Lee Potter, *New Season: The Positive Use of Commercial Television* (Columbus, OH: Charles E. Merrill, 1976).

4. Marie Winn, *The Plug-In Drug: Television, Children and the Family.* Revised edition (New York: Penguin Books, 1985).

5. Gloria Kirshner, "Positive Uses of Television" in *Television Awareness Training,* ed. Ben Logan (New York: Media Action Research Center, Inc., 1979), p. 239.

1 TV or Not TV?
And Other Good Questions

Finding out why TV is watched, understanding the needs it fulfills and questioning its effects are basic starting points for any discussion of television. By analyzing their own viewing habits and the habits of people around them, students can begin to examine their relationships with the medium to determine whether they really enjoy what they watch or whether they watch merely out of habit. They can also begin to understand the effects TV viewing has on the attitudes they develop and the ways they behave.

A TV QUESTIONNAIRE

Can your students imagine surviving a week without television? Do they think those hours they spend in front of the TV set have any effect on them?

The TV questionnaire below can help students answer such questions for themselves. The questionnaire also serves as an introduction to many of the topics addressed later in this book, and it can be used again at the end of the year to see if viewing habits or attitudes have changed. Questions can be modified for use by students of any age.

Figure 1.1: A TV Questionnaire

TV QUESTIONNAIRE

A.   Why You Watch TV

Assign a word (frequently, sometimes, rarely, never) to each of the following reasons why you watch TV:

1. For entertainment
2. For information (e.g., news, documentaries)
3. Because there is nothing better to do
4. To have something to talk about with friends
5. To learn about human relationships
6. For company (to be with others who are watching TV)
7. To get away from people
8. To forget problems
9. To be in someone else's shoes (identify with winners and sympathize with losers)
10. For instruction (e.g., educational programs)
11. For the commercials
12. Other _____

B. Personal Viewing Habits

Answer each of the following questions:

1. Estimate how much time you spend watching TV, then keep a record of your actual viewing time for a week.

- How do the results of your record compare with your original estimate?
- How do the results of your record compare with the average number of hours U.S. households watch TV (7 hours and 10 minutes per day, over a 40-hour week)?[1]
- How does the number of hours you watch TV compare with the number of hours you are asleep, in school or involved in other activities?
- Do you think you watch too much TV?

2. Do you automatically turn the TV set on when you get up in the morning or when you enter your home?

- Do you watch TV until the time you go to sleep at night?

3. Do you select what you watch carefully, or do you watch anything that's on?

- Do TV reviews ever effect your choices?

4. When you turn on the TV without a particular program in mind (just to see what's on) what do you do?

- Look for something interesting?
- Look for something familiar?
- Wait to see what's coming?
- Check the listings?
- Watch any program that follows because you don't want to change channels?

Figure 1.1: A TV Questionnaire (Cont.)

5. What do you do when a program is over?

- Turn off the TV set?
- Wait to see what's coming?
- Check the listings?
- Watch any program that follows because you don't want to change channels?
- When you do change channels, do you change because the program you were watching was bad or because something offended you?

6. Do you ever think about or discuss with others what you liked or disliked about a program?

7. Do you do your homework, eat, play a musical instrument, or do anything else while watching TV?

8. Have you ever rushed through your homework or some other activity in order to watch a particular show?

9. How often do you schedule activities around programs so you won't miss the program?

- Frequently?
- Sometimes?
- Rarely?

10. When you walk into a room where a TV set is on, do you automatically sit down to watch?

11. When a friend comes over, do you ever suggest watching TV?

- Have you ever wanted to say something to a friend but didn't because you were watching TV?

C. Family Viewing Habits

Answer each of the following questions:

1. Does the TV set occupy a prominent place in your home?

2. How often do other members of your family watch TV? Rate the amount of their viewing:

- High
- Medium
- Low

3. How selective are members of your family about what they watch on TV?

- Do they plan ahead by checking the daily or weekly listings?

4. Does your family usually watch TV together?

- If yes, do you ever talk while the program is on or discuss what you have seen?

5. How often do adults in your family watch the same programs as the children?

- Usually
- Sometimes
- Rarely

6. Is TV a major source of conflict in your home?

- In what way?

Figure 1.1: A TV Questionnaire (Cont.)

7. Does your family have rules regarding TV viewing?

   • What are they?

8. If you have younger brothers or sisters, do your parents use the TV as a baby-sitter?

9. Do your parents use TV as a reward or punishment?

10. Does the TV set stay on even if no one is watching?

11. How would you regulate viewing for a younger brother or sister?

   • Would you let them watch whatever and whenever they wanted?
   • Would you restrict their viewing to certain hours, programs or channels?
   • Would you allow them to watch TV during meal times, before school or after 10:00 p.m.?
   • Would you allow them to watch TV only on the weekends, or after chores or homework had been completed?
   • Would you check the listings first before making a decision?
   • Would you get rid of the TV set?

12. How many TV sets does your family own?

13. Does your family subscribe to cable?

   • If so, do you watch more or less TV as a result of having cable?

14. If you have a videocassette recorder (VCR), how has that affected your viewing habits?

D. How TV Affects You

Answer the following questions:

1. How much of your day's activities center around TV?

   • Have you talked about any programs or TV characters?
   • Did you miss an episode of a soap opera and ask someone what happened?
   • Did TV influence any decisions you made concerning the way you arranged your social schedule?
   • Are you wearing or carrying anything that is related to TV (stickers, books, pictures, style of dress)?
   • Have you imitated a TV character's manner of speech or movement?
   • Have you eaten any products because you saw them advertised on TV?
   • Have you sung any jingles or hummed any series' themes?
   • Are you reading a book based on a TV movie or miniseries?
   • Have you compared anything about yourself or the way you live to lifestyles you have seen on TV?
   • Do you read magazines about TV stars?
   • Do you read *TV Guide*?
   • Do you read the TV listings in the newspaper before you read the news?
   • Did you get today's news from TV?

2. Do you think you learn anything from TV?

   • Give examples.

Figure 1.1: A TV Questionnaire (Cont.)

3. Are you ever upset because a program you like has been pre-empted?

4. Do programs that follow the same pattern each week relax you?

- If they do, why?
- Is there a comfortable predictability and familiarity about the weekly cycle of programs?

5. Has TV influenced the way you feel about yourself?

- Other people?
- The United States?
- Other countries?

6. Have you ever wanted something you saw on TV and felt bad because you couldn't have it?

7. Have you stopped participating in any activities (hobbies, games, sports, reading) because you watch TV?

E. Essay Questions

1. Write an essay entitled "TV: Who Needs It?" Include your own arguments for and/or against the abolishment of TV.

2. Write about why you would like to be a particular TV character.

3. Do you like what's shown on TV? What would you change? Write an essay that includes examples of programs you watch regularly or have seen recently that you think are good or bad. If you think most of what is presented on TV is bad, indicate why you watch those programs anyway.

4. Discuss why you think TV programs are getting better or worse. Include programs you no longer watch. Talk about whether they have become too silly, unrealistic, repetitive or unfunny, or how the quality has decreased.

5. Write about a particular program you liked that was taken off the air. Include reasons why you think it should be put back on the air.

6. Are there any programs on the networks that you feel were created only for adults? Write an essay on how your younger brothers and sisters would be affected if they watched these programs.

7. Do you ever have trouble remembering what you watch on TV (especially what you saw the night before)? Have you ever started to watch a TV show and not been sure whether or not you had already seen it? If so, write an essay about why you think this happens. Include a discussion of whether you remember more of the things you have read or more of the things you have seen on TV.

COLD TURKEY: THE TV DIET

Early childhood educators have noticed a change in the behavior patterns of children. For some children, the level of violent play has increased; for others, there has been a growth of passive and withdrawn behavior. Teachers who have taught for many years report that children's play is no longer as rich, imaginative or spontaneous as it was in the past. Some professionals are attributing these changes in behavior to an increase in the amount of television that children watch, the amount of violence children see on TV (see Chapter 8), and the fact that TV viewing is a passive experience.

In one experiment, sponsored by *Redbook* magazine, in New Milford, CT children were put on a "TV diet" to see if a reduction in their TV viewing time would make a difference in their behavior and family life. For a four-week period parents cut their children's TV viewing time to no more than one hour each day. At first, the children experienced "withdrawal pangs;" they were cranky, fidgety and nervous. Parents said it was like losing a baby-sitter. After the first week, however, the children generally became more outgoing and began to engage in more activities with their parents. They increasingly relied on their imaginations during play rather than on imitations of what they had seen on TV. Communications among all family members were livelier—not because TV itself is evil—but because what had taken place, direct involvement and exploration, was more valuable.[2] In similar experiments, such as one conducted at the Horace Mann School for Nursery Years in New York City, children whose TV viewing time had been reduced appeared to be calmer, more relaxed, less easily distracted and more creative at school, and more inventive in their play (e.g., some youngsters reinvented the types of running games children had played for generations before).[3]

QUESTIONS AND ACTIVITIES

To find out what effects a TV reducing diet would have on students, ask your class to give up watching TV entirely for one week. If students are reluctant to go "cold turkey" they can analyze their feelings by completing statements such as, "I need TV to..." or "Without TV I would..." Discuss addictions with your students. Signs of an addiction include the following:

1. Experiencing a "high" that normal life does not supply.
2. Dependence upon a certain experience, an increased inability to function normally without it, and the need to repeat the experience again and again.[4]

Ask students if they think they are addicted to TV. Suggest that they limit their viewing, for a one-week period, to a few specials or programs they really look forward to. Ask them to stop watching TV completely during the following week. During this week, the "no-TV week," students should record their feelings, thoughts and activities in a daily journal.

• At the end of the week, discuss the experiment (students may want to read passages aloud directly from their journals). Questions for class discussion follow:

Did students find it as hard as they thought it would be to go without TV?
Did anyone cheat? If they did cheat, was it because someone else was watching TV and they couldn't resist? Was it because they were confined indoors? Was it because they wanted to watch the news? Maybe it was because the TV set was just *there*?
How often did students have to stop themselves from reaching automatically for the dial?

How many times did they find themselves automatically turning their heads toward the TV set when it was on?

- Family members must have been affected by this experiment.

  Ask students if they were able to involve anyone else in the experiment.
  Find out if they talked more or did more things with their families during the "no-TV week."
  Were they teased or taunted by brothers and sisters who tried to get them to watch TV by making everything on the set sound exciting?
  Did students feel left out when other members of their families were watching TV and they weren't?

- Faced with extra time on their hands, how did the students occupy themselves:

  Did they read?
  Play an instrument?
  Listen to the radio?
  Try something they never tried before?
  Would students be willing to try the experiment again?
  Do they think reducing the amount of time they spend watching TV could improve the quality of their lives?

- Colleagues who teach other grade levels may be interested in trying the experiment. Results will probably vary according to the age group of the students involved. Conclusions drawn from the questionnaire should be taken into consideration when the experiment is evaluated. It should be noted that students who find the TV diet easy may already be watching very little TV.

- Students may not be aware of how recent the phenomenon of TV addiction is. Suggest that they ask their parents and grandparents what activities they pursued when they were children. Other questions to ask include:

Did students' parents and grandparents have TV in their homes when they were growing up?
If not, how were their lives different?
What did they do after supper or on Saturday mornings?
How did they find out about the news?
When they did get a TV, how did it change their lives?

CONCLUSION

Journals of children, ages thirteen and below, who participated in a no-TV experiment conducted in the late 1970s by *Children's Express* (a magazine written and edited by children), showed that the week without TV was the slowest week they had ever experienced. The children reported having feelings of "aimlessness" and "eerieness." Many said they wanted to watch *anything* just for reassurance or to get rid of occasional "scary feelings." They felt left out and wanted to cheat by watching TV in a store or at a friend's house. One 12-year-old summed up her feelings by writing, "I am having a hard struggle . . . but I'll be OK. It's not like I'm breaking out in hives or anything." Another child simply stated, "I'm beyond help."[5]

Entries also showed that because children were not rushing to see a TV program, they relaxed more; they listened to the radio, cleaned their rooms and "luxuriated in the bathtub."

Experiments in which entire families have turned off the TV set have demonstrated that, although TV was missed, most families felt they had benefited from the experience. In Denver, CO in 1974, for example, 15 families turned off their TV sets for a month. After a "withdrawal" period, parents and children reported missing TV less and less. They sought active things to do alone and with each other; children read more, helped with household chores and played outdoors. Overall, parents noted a greater feeling of closeness and a more peaceful atmosphere in the home.[6]

One unanticipated result of a no-TV experiment occurred in Providence, RI. In an attempt to give students a new perspective on the place of television in their lives, the chairman of the English department at the Wheeler School invited families to participate in a month-long "Television Challenge." The rules stipulated that for the entire month of November, TV was not to be watched by any individual member of the family at any time or for any reason. The family could, however, elect to watch one program per week together. This program was to be agreed upon by unanimous vote. Surprisingly, several parents reported that, unlike previous years, their children never mentioned Christmas during the entire month of November.[7]

NOTES

1. John Naisbitt, "Trendnotes," *San Francisco Chronicle* (8 April, 1986), p. 2.
2. Claire Safran, "How TV Changes Children," in *Television Awareness Training,* ed. Ben Logan (New York: Media Action Research Center, 1979), pp. 227–230, passim.
3. Ibid. p. 228.
4. Marie Winn, *The Plug-In Drug: Television, Children, and the Family,* rev. ed. (New York: Penguin, 1985), pp. 23–24.
5. Dorriet Kavanaugh, ed., *Listen to Us! The Children's Express Report* (New York: Workman, 1978), pp. 163–172 passim.
6. Marie Winn, *The Plug-In Drug,* pp. 247–250.
7. Peggy Charren and Martin W. Sandler, *Changing Channels: Living (Sensibly) with Television* (Reading, MA: Addison-Wesley, 1983), p. 190.

2 The Three Rs: Ratings, Revenues and Regulations

Very often TV series appear in the seasonal schedules only to be canceled. Why do many programs devoid of intelligent writing, believable plots or realistic characters enjoy a successful run on television while other programs of better quality struggle to make it through the season, if they even make it that far?

What we see on TV, when we see it and whether we see it at all depend on many factors. The interests of the sponsors, the results of polls, the current climate of opinion, what competing networks are doing and certain conventional formats all determine what gets on, and stays on, the air. Most programming decisions are based on what will attract and hold the largest audience, thus generating the largest revenues. The success of a program generally has little to do with its quality.

Ratings get the most consideration when decisions are made as to what stays and goes on TV. In order not to be canceled, a network program needs to attract over 25 million viewers on a single night. Theoretically, the larger the audience, the more people advertisers can reach and the greater the profits for both advertisers and networks. According to David Poltrack, director of research for the CBS Broadcasting Group in New York, a gain of a single rating point during prime time could mean $65 million more in advertising revenues for a network over the period of a year.[1]

Unfortunately, TV ratings don't report on what people would like to be watching, how much they enjoy what they do watch or if they are even paying attention. The 1200 Nielsen family homes represent only .0003 of the American population, and the statistics used by broadcasters measure only the stations TV sets are tuned in to, not who is watching. A dog watching TV alone could represent the viewing habits of about half a million Americans.[2]

Other polls are often used to determine audience preferences and may be interpreted to show what the pollster or promotion department wants them to show. When 10 people are asked which of three particular programs is their favorite (without the option of saying "none"), the answer could be interpreted to mean that the respondent likes the chosen show, even if it was named because it was the least offensive of the three. A pollster could, for example, take a poll of TV show preferences at an automobile showroom and use the results to say that 9 out of 10 viewers in a recent survey chose "My Mother the Car" as the show they liked best. If the people surveyed did like the show they might not be representative of a larger number who didn't.

Another factor that influences what we see on TV is government regulation. The major regulatory agency, the Federal Communications Commission (FCC), was established in 1934 to oversee radio and television broadcasts, and to ensure that the public interest is served in exchange for free use of the airwaves by broadcasters. The effectiveness of the FCC and the amount of control it should have has been debated ever since. Critics claim that the public interest standard has never been successfully enforced; that private citizens don't have the time or money to counter the efforts of broadcasters lobbying the FCC and other agencies; that since FCC chairmen are presidential appointees their attitudes reflect those of the administration in office; and that the FCC seems to be friendlier to the broadcast industry than it is to the public.

One recent example of a controversy surrounds an FCC decision focused on several TV guidelines. FCC guidelines originally required TV stations to present a certain minimum number of news and public affairs programs. The guidelines also limited the number of commercials a station could air each hour and required a TV station to learn about the community in which it operated to determine what types of programming would be the most beneficial. In 1984, these regulations were abolished. As a result, stations no longer have to reserve at least 10% of their air time for nonentertainment programs and at least half of that for news and public affairs programs Other regulations no longer in effect include requirements that 5% of all programs be locally produced or that the total amount of time allotted for ads be limited to 16 minutes per hour. Stations are also no longer required to maintain, and keep available for public inspection, logs of all the programs they present on the air.

Some agency officials felt the action would have little immediate impact since most stations already exceeded federal standards for news and public affairs programs and fell short of the FCC commercial time limit. They claimed competition could be relied on to keep stations from broadcasting excessive advertising. Officials also felt the ruling would eliminate paper work for station owners and was another step forward for public freedom, where viewers (rather than the government) would decide what *they* want to watch on TV. Deregulation may also make it harder for stations to have their FCC licenses renewed every five years. Merely meeting the former standards will no longer assure renewal, and proving that programming is in the public interest may be more difficult.

Critics claim that the broadcasting system is being turned over to commercial interests. They fear that the quality of programming will decline and that without guidelines stations will not schedule local interest programs. They believe the abolition of program logs will leave the public with no way to monitor a station's performance, and that stations will be tempted to use less expensive programming, such as old movies and syndicated shows, rather than new programs produced in their studios. It is also feared that there will be a reduction in the number of children's programs aired.

QUESTIONS AND ACTIVITIES

By pretending to control and regulate TV programming, students can gain a better understanding of the factors involved in the selection, writing and scheduling of programs. They will also gain insight into why certain programs, regardless of their quality, are picked up or canceled by the networks. They will see why certain subjects are not covered on TV and why each new season is pretty much the same as the last.

Pollstergeists

To help students gain an understanding of the TV rating system, a variety of class activities can be developed around TV polls.

• Turn your class into a "ratings family." In the A.C. Nielsen system (the best known of TV ratings systems), a rating is the percentage of total TV households watching a particular show; a share is the percentage of TV households with their TV sets turned on and tuned to that show. Survey the class to find out how many students have a TV set (TV households). Then determine how many TVs were turned on at a particular time and which programs they were tuned in to. (If 20 of your 30 TV households had their TVs on and 10 were tuned to a particular program, then that program would receive a 50% share or one-half of 20.)

Discuss why students were watching that program. Perhaps they were watching because the program happened to be on before or after a program they really liked. Maybe they were tuned to that program because other members of the family wanted to watch it, or because there was nothing better on. If they liked the program, have them defend their choice by giving valid criticisms and explanations of what they objected to in competing programs (if they've seen them). Determine the shares for programs broadcast at other hours and on other days, then post the results:

Give each program a rank from 1 to 10 based on its share.
List the ten most popular programs for that week (Monday through Sunday).
Indicate whether each program was a premiere (P), movie (M), repeat (R) or
    special (S). Use an asterisk (*) to indicate ties.
Indicate the network the program appeared on.

Repeat the poll over a period of several weeks to see if the same programs win the same share of viewers. Program popularity may shift from one week to another or a special program could beat the regulars in the ratings.

• Divide the class into groups. Have each group conduct a poll that asks questions such as these:

What is your favorite TV program?
What is your favorite *type* of program?
Who are your favorite TV characters?

Students can poll other students, friends, family members or people in the community. Tabulate the results and plot one or more graphs. Based on the results of the poll, pose the following questions:

Ask students how misleading or representative they think the results are.
Do they think the questions were objective?
Do they see any differences in the answers given by males and females?
Ask them to determine whether one sex tends to watch more of one kind of program than the other.
Are there differences in responses among age groups?

• Since different programs are popular in different regions of the country, pollsters often identify who is watching particular programs in cities such as Los Angeles, San Francisco, Chicago and New York. Try something similar by having students take a poll of students in different grades to find out which programs are most popular in those grades. Post the results so students throughout the school can see what their peers watch. Students might want to update the survey each month to see which programs gain or lose popularity.

• Students can bring in examples of statistics they think are misleading. These can be obtained from TV or printed materials.

To help students understand how and why statistics are often misleading, create a questionnaire for a poll based on a topic of the students' choice. Word it so that it will yield the results they want. Post the results with an attached note that asks its readers to identify what is misleading or being misrepresented in the statistics.

Program Schedules and Formats

Programs are scheduled from a variety of standard sources (see Figure 2.1). There are also several standard sources that are used for developing new programs.

Figure 2.1: Types and Methods of Programming

The basic types of programs are adventures, comedies, dramas, documentaries, educational programs, game shows, cartoons, news and sports programs, soap operas, talk shows and variety programs. During the course of a day, TV stations broadcast programs from numerous sources. Regularly scheduled local programs (news, public affairs and entertainment) make up about 10% of an average station's broadcasting; network programming makes up about 60%; and syndicated programming accounts for approximately 30%.

Local News originates live from the TV studio and is supplemented with videotaped or filmed recordings.

Public Affairs programs are a local programming priority. These shows cover subjects and issues that affect the community within a station's broadcasting range. They never earn as much money as their production costs the station, and they attract relatively small audiences and, therefore, little advertising. Public affairs programs are presented live, or taped as studio talk shows (usually the most cost-effective format).

Documentaries can be produced by TV stations, filmed or taped. They inform rather than entertain and frequently address subjects already identified by other news sources. A good documentary presents an important problem and the elements contributing to it. It may or may not offer solutions. Cultural and historical subjects are also explored by documentaries to help communities view their changes and development.

Entertainment programs are frequently acquired from networks or independent production houses. Local TV entertainment programs are usually confined to sports, talent competitions, variety/talk shows and children's programs.

Network Programming includes national news, situation comedies, dramas, soap operas, game shows, sports and children's programs. The network provides affiliates with programs they could never afford to produce themselves. The stations reciprocate by permitting wide distribution of the network's commercial messages.

The networks actually own very few programs beyond news and public affairs broadcasts. Almost all entertainment programming is owned by sponsors or independent production studios which sell the rights-to-broadcast to the network but not the programs themselves. In effect, networks choose their entertainment programs from a broad file of competitors, encourage or discourage the development of a series, and "rent" the use of that series (or movie) for a certain period of time. After that, rights to the property are either renegotiated or given up.

The affiliated station receives the program from the network, adds local and national spot advertising to the network commercials and sends the program to the local audience. Sometimes stations delay broadcasting by taping a program and airing it later. Occasionally, a station may choose not to air a program at all.

Syndicated Programs are usually taken from a series that was popular on a particular network. Off network syndication refers to programs that have previously gone off the air, and that have been sold to individual stations around the country by a syndicator who was hired by the original owner.

Products of original syndication are programs that have been sold to individual stations or small groups of stations but which have not been previously shown on a network. These programs may include some pre-sold commercials which help to defray production

Figure 2.1. Types and Methods of Programming (Cont.)

costs for the syndicator. Although the station derives no income from these commercials and they reduce the amount of advertising time available for local sales, pre-sold commercials are tolerated by many stations because they make good programs affordable.

Barter syndication is similar to original syndication except that barter programs are underwritten by an advertiser and include at least two minutes of commercials. These programs are given to stations free of charge. The station reciprocates by not charging for the advertising time used by the sponsor(s).

Source: Adapted from *The Television Picture,* CBS Television Network. Copyright © CBS Television Network, 1981.

Last Season's Successes

● Every few years, TV schedules seem to be dominated by one particular type of program. Popular themes have included westerns, medical programs and programs that intertwine multiple stories and characters.

Students might enjoy looking through books that list TV schedules for previous years to see what types of programs were popular at different times. While students are going over this material, ask them to consider questions such as these:

Which type of program seems to be most popular during the current TV season?
Why were certain programs popular at different times?
Have there been any cycles in the popularity of themes over the years?
Does there appear to be any particular reason why westerns (for example) have not been popular in the last few years?
What types of programs have always been popular?

● Spinoffs of popular TV shows also play a role in program scheduling. Have students create TV family trees or diagrams that show current programs that are spinoffs of other series. If students can recall spinoffs from the last five years, have them diagram these also. Following are further questions for students to explore:

What was the first spinoff in TV history?
Are there currently more TV spinoffs than there were five years ago? If yes, what are the reasons?
Based on past TV schedules, were spinoffs more popular during some seasons than during others? What are the reasons?
What makes certain characters more appropriate for starring roles in spinoffs than others?
What characters would students choose to star in a spinoff series?
What qualities make these characters appealing?
Which characters do students think would not make good subjects for spinoffs?

The Amazing Spiderman character based upon a popular children's comic strip.

Great Expectations

• Movies also make their way into TV program schedules. Have students think about films they've seen recently. Ask them to reflect on which of these would make a good TV series. When students have selected a film, suggest that they make a list of characters and their traits. Then, as a written assignment, have students prepare story outlines for three episodes of a TV series based on the film.

• Characters from comic strips are often used in cartoons or portrayed by actors on television. Many children are especially fond of comic strip superheroes because these characters can do things children would like to be able to do.

Students can choose a comic strip character they admire and develop a class discussion from the following questions:

What do students like about the character?
What kind of value system does the character have?
What things would the character *never* do?
How does the character act, speak and move?
What does the character frequently say?
Where (what places) would the character most often be found?

Based on information gained from the above discussion, have students write an outline for the first episode of a new series starring the character. Students may want to act this out at a later time.

Program Formulas

• After identifying program formulas (see Figure 2.2), ask students to look for examples of top spin, heat, pipe, hooks and blows in the programs they watch. Ask students to think about whether program formulas restrict the range of motivation, characterization and plot that can be developed. Also discuss whether these formulas can provide a comfortable predictability and familiarity that will keep viewers watching week after week.

• Divide the class into groups. Have each group write and act out a scene that follows the rule of "least objectionable programming" (see Figure 2.2). While each group acts out its scene, have the rest of the class make notes about anything that might be considered objectionable. Discuss whether the views presented in the scene are consistent with current popular views.

Station to Station: Programming and Advertisers

Divide the class into three groups—one to form a company that has a line of products to sell, and two to form competing TV stations. Each station should invent its own call letters, logo and schedule of programs for one week. (These can be developed

Figure 2.2: Program Formulas

> Writers follow certain conventions that have nothing to do with motivation, characterization or plot. The formula follows:
>
> 1. Each dramatic scene should have **top spin**—enough excitement to push the audience into the next scene.
>
> 2. Each dramatic scene should have **heat**—a tense, emotional moment that will keep the audience interested in the show.
>
> 3. When a new character appears on a familiar show, or a new show premiers, each character or situation should be provided with **pipe**—background leading to the point where the character enters or situation begins. Some programs provide **pipe** at the beginning of each program, usually during the opening credits.
>
> 4. The beginning of the program and the opening of each segment after a commercial break should have a **hook**—i.e., a situation that will catch the viewers' attention and create (or sustain) the viewers' interest in the program.
>
> 5. In a comedy, a character leaving a scene has to exit with a **blow** or **button**—a joke.
>
> 6. In a TV sitcom, characters should always be talking, and every other sentence should be funny. It doesn't matter whether or not the characters are listening to each other, as long as they say something.
>
> 7. Conflicts must be resolved by the end of the show even if it means using contrived plots, unbelievable situations and amazing character transformations to achieve the resolution.
>
> 8. TV schedules should follow the principle of **least objectionable programming**. Researchers claim that people don't watch specific programs—they watch *TV,* and they don't change channels unless something offends or upsets them. Audiences are content with familiar ideas and convictions. To provide the best possible climate for the ads, controversy should be avoided at all costs.

Sources: Michael Kelley's *A Parents' Guide to Television* (John Wiley and Sons, 1983) and Donna Cross's *Media-Speak* (Mentor/New American Library, 1983).

as ideas for the beginning of a new TV season.) Students can invent completely new program titles and descriptions, or base their programs on ones already being broadcast. As students create their schedules, they should consider the following:

● Program schedules are based on audience interest. Students should think about who watches TV during the day and who is likely to tune in around dinner time, during the family hour (8 to 9:00 p.m.) and late at night. (Point out that an evening's programs—from 7:00 p.m. to 12:00 midnight—may contain as many as 5 one-hour shows or 10 half-hour shows.)

● New or weak programs do better in polls if they are scheduled between two strong programs or preceded by a popular one.

● Documentaries don't usually draw as large an audience as entertainment programs. If students want to schedule a documentary, they should think about when they could attract the largest number of viewers. They should also consider what kinds of documentaries should be scheduled at specific times of the year, such as during sweeps week, when ratings become especially important.

● The FCC considers the inclusion of children's programs to be "generally required for programming in the public interest."[3] Where would students place these programs in the schedule so children would be likely to see them? Why might they want to "bury" the programs in a time slot when children wouldn't be likely to watch (e.g., late afternoon, dinner time or Saturday afternoon—when children are involved in other activities)?

● Stations are also required by the FCC to provide public service announcements. Keeping in mind that these announcements don't bring revenue into the station, ask students where they think these segments should be scheduled. Also discuss what types of public service announcements they would want to run.

● Programs are subject to censorship by the station manager. What restrictions should students place on the types of programs they show? (Remind students that their "station" is accountable to their teacher, parents, school adminstration and community for renewal of its license and permission to air its programs.)

● Programming is also subject to the station's budget. Students might want to research and approximate the budget of a small TV station. (Both class stations should start with the same budget.)

When the schedules have been completed, have students from each station look at the other's schedule. After they have examined each other's programs, they may want to make changes on their own schedules. (For example, is the opposing station planning to show a blockbuster movie when they are planning reruns?)

Both stations should then prepare an outline of their advertising rates before presenting their program schedules to the "company" (third group of students), for inspection. Students will find the following guidelines helpful when setting their fees:

> Currently, a sponsor can be charged $300,000 for a 30-second ad on a highly rated series; the same ad on a new program given little chance of success may cost $60,000 to $70,000. McDonald's spends about $130 million a year on TV advertising, with General Foods averaging $80 million, AT&T $50 million and Honda $30 million.[4]

The company must consider what kinds of advertising the stations will accept, and how much they charge per minute for advertising time on their programs. They will need to know whether the same amount is charged for all products, programs and time periods.

While the stations try to sell advertising time to the company, the company must set its own budget and determine which programs would receive the largest and most appropriate audiences for its advertisements. This can be done by distributing copies of both TV station schedules to the entire class. Poll students to find out which programs would receive the largest viewing audiences.

Advise the company that for this activity the same product cannot be advertised on both stations during the same time period. Students will have to choose the program that they feel best meets their needs. After negotiations have been completed, it will be easy to determine which station accumulates the most advertising time.

Foreign Markets

In 1984, CBS and China Central Television announced the airing of the first regularly scheduled broadcasts of American television in the People's Republic of China. The following programs were selected by a delegation of Chinese officials:[5]

- Drama
The House Without a Christmas Tree, a 1972 drama about a 10-year-old farm girl whose widowed father wouldn't allow her to have a Christmas tree because it would remind him of his departed wife.

- News/Documentaries
Selections from *60 Minutes* and *On the Road.*
Charles Kuralt's vignettes of Americana.
Episodes from a Walter Cronkite historical series on World War II.

- Sports
Quarterback Princess, a TV movie about a girl's struggle to join her high school's all-male football team.
Superskates, an ice extravaganza.
The Iditarod, the story of a grueling, 12-day dogsled race from Anchorage to Nome, Alaska.
Selections from NBA basketball, NCAA football and boxing.

Students may find it interesting to choose a foreign country and research its history, culture, economics and political system. Based on the information gained, a TV program schedule could be developed for that country for one day. Students can decide which American programs they would or would not want the people of that country to see. Programs that might be offensive and political material, documentaries or scientific reports that would be unsuitable for overseas broadcast could be listed.

Public Access and the FCC

Neither stations nor networks own the airwaves. The FCC regulates access to TV airwaves, and it requires that TV stations assure their fair use by the public. There are three categories of public access rights:[6]

1. The equal time provision requires equal opportunities for all political candidates for the same office to campaign on a station.
2. The Fairness Doctrine requires broadcasters to provide reasonable opportunities for the presentation of conflicting viewpoints concerning controversial issues of public importance.
3. The right of rebuttal entitles persons or groups to respond when their honesty, character or integrity have been attacked.

The following activities and questions are suggested to encourage class participation and discussion of public access regulations:

*   What are the requirements of each of the above provisions? (Research and report.)
*   What problems have these provisions given rise to?
*   How much control do the media have within each of these provisions?
*   Have there been any efforts made toward reform?
*   Can the equal time rule be circumvented?
*   What might happen if a group with an opposing view to a controversial program wanted to air its view under the Fairness Doctrine?
*   How would individuals go about obtaining time to present their views on TV?

Other areas to explore:

*   The responsibilities of the FCC
*   Current FCC members and how they are selected
*   The periodic TV licensing renewal process
*   How politicians are granted political air time
*   Presidential air time
*   How the FCC protects access rights for low revenue programming such as children's programs, classical music programs and programs directed toward minority audiences

CONCLUSION

Now that students have had the opportunity to place themselves in the position of program manager and with their new knowledge gained from the above exercises, students can summarize their feelings about TV ratings, revenues and regulations with the following questions:

- Do students feel that they currently have any control over which programs are put on the air?
- Should program content be controlled or regulated by a government agency?
- Is the periodic licensing renewal process for TV stations a good idea?
- If students owned a station but were not required to produce public service programs, would they do so out of good will toward the community?
- Should local stations be forced to produce more original programming?
- Considering the fact that commercial TV is dependent on the revenues that advertising brings in, would fear of antagonizing the public keep students from increasing the number of commercials they broadcast?
- Should viewers pay for programs they want to see but stations don't want to show because of low ratings?
- Since broadcasters use the airwaves (a public resource) to make a profit, should they be free to choose their programming?
- Should they pay for the use of the airwaves in some way other than by performing a public service?

NOTES

1. Laurie How, "Upstart Challenges TV Ratings Grants," *San Francisco Examiner* (28 July 1985): D2.

2. Glenn Alan Cheney, *Television in American Society* (New York: Franklin Watts, 1983), p. 19.

3. Stewart M. Hoover, "Television: Strategies For Change," in *Television Awareness Training,* ed. Ben Logan (Abingdon/Nashville, 1979), p. 117.

4. Mark Lacter, "The Advertisers Have Mysteries to Solve Too," *San Francisco Chronicle* (11 September 1985).

5. Terrence O'Flaherty," CBS Feeds the Dragon," *San Francisco Examiner* (5 August 1984, "TV Week"): 3.

6. Section 315 of the Federal Communication Act of 1934. Doris Graber, *Mass Media and American Politics* (Washington, D.C.: Congressional Quarterly Press, 1980), p. 91.

3 Television and Language Arts

Studies have demonstrated that too much TV viewing can contribute to lower reading scores among school-age children. In 1980, for example, 99% of students in California in the 6th and 12th grades were evaluated for achievement in areas that included reading and written expression. Assessment of the results found that as students' daily hours of TV viewing increased, scores for both grades in both areas decreased. The declines in achievement scores held for all socioeconomic strata with the exception of sixth grade pupils with limited English language ability.[1] Another study conducted two years later by the California State Department of Education yielded similar results (see Table 3.1). In this study 500,000 6th and 12th graders were evaluated. Again, those who watched the most TV did poorest in the state's achievement tests.[2]

A study conducted by George Gerbner of school children in New Jersey also supports these findings. In this study, heavy TV watchers scored lower on achievement tests measuring school-learned skills and on IQ tests designed to measure basic intelligence. The only exceptions were heavy TV watchers from the very lowest family income levels, who tended to score higher than those low-income students who watched little or no TV. Based on his findings, Gerbner suggests that a student who does well on tests is typically one who does a great deal of reading and who is engaged "in a variety of different and stimulating activities. A student like that is a light television watcher partially because of everything else he is doing. . . .Heavy viewing displaces these activities and this has a flattening effect on [the student's test scores]."[3]

Researchers don't actually draw a cause-and-effect relationship between TV viewing and scholastic achievement; nor do they say that all children who watch large amounts of TV do badly on tests. What the research does suggest, however, is that heavy TV viewers who get above-average scores on achievement tests could score even higher if they did not watch as much television.

Table 3.1: How Watching TV Affects Grades

Hours of TV per weekday	Reading	Writing
None	73	71
0 – 1/2	75	74
1/2 – 1	74	72
1 – 2	73	72
2 – 3	73	70
3 – 4	72	70
4 – 5	71	68
5 – 6	70	68
6 +	66	64

Source: Copyright © *San Francisco Chronicle*, 21 July 1982. Reprinted by permission.

QUESTIONS AND ACTIVITIES

Even though TV viewing is a passive activity that does not encourage reading or written or oral expression, TV and its related materials can be used as constructive teaching tools to heighten your class's language arts skills.

TV listings can be a valuable starting point for building vocabulary as well as a vehicle for teaching how information is categorized and summarized. TV scripts have many of the same elements found in plays, short stories and novels and can be used to teach character development, creation of settings, themes, plots, conflicts and resolutions.

The following activities, while encouraging students to become more critical TV viewers, can help them to develop their oral and written expression skills. They can also be used to teach grammar and comprehension and to promote independent reading.

Using TV Listings

Class Act

• As discussed in Chapter 2, the FCC asks TV stations to broadcast certain types of programs to serve the public's interests, needs and desires. These programs can follow numerous topics and themes. Have students look at the programs scheduled for a week on a single channel and classify them according to the following types of programming:[4]

Entertainment (situation comedies, drama, action/adventure, variety, made-for-
TV movies, theatrical films)
Programs that display local talent
Children's programs
Religious programs
Educational programs
Public affairs programs
Editorials by licensees
Political broadcasts
Agricultural programs
News programs
Weather and market reports
Sports programs
Minority audience programs

Roots and Definitions

TV Guide magazine or the entertainment section of a local periodical can be a valuable starting point for several language arts activities that involve vocabulary building and development of writing skills.

• After pointing out that locating the day of the week and air time of a particular program is similar to using guide words to locate specific words in a dictionary, have students start their own dictionaries. Students can use the TV listings to obtain words for which they don't know the meanings or that are specific to TV. Abbreviations such as **ABC, NBC, CBS** and **FCC** can be used. Entries in the students' dictionaries should indicate the part of speech as well as the definition of the word.

• Explore the etymology of media-related words such as:

Anchorman, named for the person on the end of the rope in a game of tug o' war.
Television, from the Greek—tele for "far away" and Latin—videre for "to see."

• Identify words with the same root or prefix (e.g., telephone, telekinesis, tele-conference, telecommunications). Create sentence completion games for the class by writing the root of the media-related word at the top of the page followed by unfinished sentences that require a word based on that root to be filled in. An example is given below:

tele

1. Students in cities and towns across the nation can see and talk to each other simultaneously through the use of **telecommunications.**

2. Some people claim they can move objects without touching them, just by thinking about it. This process is called **telekinesis**.

• To develop vocabulary skills students can complete the crossword puzzles that appear in the *TV Guide*. They can also create their own crossword puzzles, and as a variation design word search puzzles.

Word search puzzles are produced by first making a list of media-related words. These words are then hidden in a grid of letters. Words can be spelled backwards or forwards, horizontally, vertically or diagonally in the grid. To create a more challenging puzzle, the unused letters can be used to spell out a secret message or answer a question that is asked as part of the puzzle.

• Ask students to keep two pages of vocabulary words: one that lists words with double meanings and a second that classifies words by topics. Suggested words for the first list include those whose meanings refer to TV as well as to other topics, (medium, cast, pan, shot, subject, channel, screen, receiver, tune, star, pilot, set, etc.). The second list could relate to topics the students are studying such as "TV violence," which could include words such as conflict, resolution, aggression, etc.

• For further work with definitions, have students read the script of a TV production to locate words they don't know. (A list of organizations and stations that provide scripts for classroom use can be found in the resource section of the appendix of this book.) Students should try a variety of exercises with unfamiliar words.

1. Define the words by studying the context in which they are used.
2. Look them up in the dictionary.
3. Write the correct definitions.
4. Write synonyms.
5. Write antonyms.
6. Write sentences using the words.

Photo Story

• Photographs can be very suggestive. Have students look through periodicals for TV-related photographs. They can then write captions or brief stories about the photographs they have chosen. Suggest that students write a description of the photo from the point of view of someone—or something—in the photograph. This can be done several times, each time taken from a different point of view. A series of specific questions may help them get started:

What happened just before the photograph was taken?
What is happening now?
What action will follow?

Young students can take part in this exercise by writing a sentence about a picture. The sentence can then be broken down into its parts, i.e., the subject and the predicate. Parts of speech such as nouns, verbs, adjectives and adverbs can also be identified.

Person to Person

• Students will enjoy writing simple and complex character analogies based on character relationships in programs they are familiar with. (This can also be done using characters from a script that is read in class.) Some of the most obvious relationships to investigate are those between a husband and wife, male partners, male and female partners where there is an adversary relationship, and relationships between people of different ages or those of different social status. Another popular relationship analogy would be between superheroes and realistic characters. The following fill-in-the-blank sentence completion exercises are examples of such analogies.

Archie Bunker is to Edith Bunker as _____ is to _____ .
He-Man is to Skeletor as _____ is to _____ .
Batman is to Robin as _____ is to _____ .
Superman is to Lois Lane as _____ is to _____ .

Feedback

• Encourage students to examine the different styles of critical and descriptive annotations used in TV listings. Based on this exercise, they can write their own annotations summarizing programs they have recently watched. Remind students that in order to write the annotations, they will have to summarize and condense the action of the program in only a few words or sentences. A discussion of the following writing styles for annotations will also be helpful.

Descriptive, where the basic plot of a program is simply related.
Critical, where programs are analyzed. (Descriptive phrases from critical annotations could include "the same old characters act in the same old ways. . ." or "still funny after all these years.")
Promotional, where the show is described in such a way that viewers feel they will be missing something good if they do not watch the program.

When students have completed this assignment, discuss which programs they had the least difficulty summarizing and why. Do the same for the programs they felt were the most difficult.

Field Guide

• Create a publication based on the *TV Guide* with your class. Include editorials, reviews of TV ads (evaluate the ad itself and/or the performance of the product), puzzles, art (perhaps caricatures of performers) and programs students would recommend as good for children.

Reviews of programs should focus on the following:

How events unfolded (Did they unfold in a logical sequence?)
Character development
Dialogue
Theme (Was the message of the story clear?)
Quality of the production (To be described in terms of elements such as lighting, sound, music, acting, camera technique, sets, scenery, costumes and style of production.)

When the project is complete make copies available to students in your class, those in other classes and perhaps to members of the community. Check with local newspapers that might be interested in running a weekly review column written by students.

Belle and Sebastian, an animated series for children presented by the NICKELODEON Channel.

Photo courtesy of NICKELODEON

Using TV Scripts

As was mentioned earlier, TV scripts have many of the same elements found in plays, short stories and novels. Students can familiarize themselves, in class, with scripts for broadcast programs. They may also be interested in writing their own TV scripts to be acted out in class or videotaped and played back. Fairy and folk tales are good resources, as are poetry, fiction and nonfiction books.

The following activities are designed to teach students language arts skills such as plot and characterization of stories as well as reading comprehension and vocabulary development.

Reading Between the Lines

• Examples of literary devices can often be found in TV scripts. Using scripts chosen by your students, list as many as you can find. The following describes a few:

alliteration, repetition of the same sound at the start of a series of words
metaphor, writing or speaking figuratively and describing something in terms of something else
onomatopeia, the naming of a thing or action by a vocal imitation of the sound associated with it
personification, attributing inanimate objects or abstract notions with a personal nature or character
simile, directly expressing a resemblance, in one or more points, of one thing to another

• Identify instances of the following types of humor:

exaggeration, overstatement
irony, a contradiction between the literal and the intended meaning—i.e., saying one thing and implying another
misunderstanding, a situation arising as the result of a mistake or disagreement
pun, a play on words, the humorous use of a word to suggest two or more of its meanings, or to suggest another word similar in sound but different in meaning
put down, to disparage or insult
sarcasm, the use of a harsh or cutting tone that may be ironical or satirical
satire, the use of irony, sarcasm or ridicule for some serious purposes—e.g., exposing abuses
slapstick, broad, physical comedy in which rough play prevails
surprise, something unexpected

• Lists of words that express emotion or action, or that have been borrowed from other languages can be derived from TV scripts. These words can be categorized according to their parts of speech.

• Idioms (peculiar forms of expression—i.e., phrases that express ideas in colorful ways) can also be found in TV scripts and listed. Students can complete the following exercises:

1. Write the meaning of the idiom, along with a literal translation.
2. Illustrate or pantomime common idioms such as "losing face" or "wild goose chase," while the rest of the class tries to identify them.
3. Discuss how these expressive words help the reader to visualize action and characters.

Characterization, Plot and Setting

• List each of the major characters that appeared in a TV script or were seen in a dramatization. Then have students suggest adjectives that describe each character (what they looked like; how they acted, etc.). If a script is read before a program has been viewed, ask the class to draw or write descriptions of what they think the major characters should look like. Students can also try to identify a character by listening to a list of adjectives describing that character.

• In a written or oral assignment, students can discuss how each character in a chosen script contributed to the movement of the plot, and whether any of the characters changed in the course of the action.

• Students can select one particular character they admired and write a script based on a day's events from that character's point of view. A similar assignment can be done with a character that is not quite as popular.

• To develop comprehension skills, ask students to list, in order, the incidents that made up a particular dramatization. Draw a chart that identifies the main plot, subplots, incidents that moved the action forward to the turning point (the event that brings about the resolution) and the actual resolution. Other possible resolutions can also be included. The following questions might be offered for class discussion:

What is the central idea(s) of the story?
Is there a major theme?
What are the cause and effect relationships between specific events in the story?
What are the conflicts in the story?
How were these conflicts resolved?
What literary devices made some moments suspenseful?
If a sequel were written to the story, what would it be like?

Behind the Scenes

• To give students a feeling for the importance of settings and scenery, ask them to list, in chronological order, the various settings that appeared in a dramatization. Each setting should be described along with an account of the action that took place there. Questions for class discussion could include these:

How did the setting contribute to the mood of the story?
Did the setting reveal anything about the nature of the characters?
How did the setting help to establish the scene?

• Have students read a script before seeing the telecast: have them draw their own settings, based on the descriptions in the text.

• As a related activity, discuss the settings in photographs that have been taken at a variety of locations. Ask the following questions:

Can students identify the locations in the pictures?
If so, what details enabled them to determine where the photos were taken?
What kinds of feelings do students get from looking at the pictures?

Literary License

Often, when a short story or novel is adapted for TV, many things are changed. To help students understand how and why this happens, ask the class to watch a TV program that has been based on a previously published short story or novel. The class should also read the story or book upon which the TV production was based. When this aspect of the assignment has been completed, elements of the story such as characterization, plot, dialogue, settings, motivation and relationships among characters should be analyzed and a comparison drawn between the two media. To promote class discussion ask questions such as these:

Since the TV production is a condensed version of the original, what details were left out?
How did hearing characters speak directly with one another differ from reading dialogue? How did watching the action differ from reading about it in the narration?
What are the limitations of adapting a story to video?
What are the advantages?
If students were to produce their own version of the written story for TV, what aspects of the story would they leave out?
What aspects would they leave in?

At this point students might be interested in writing their own script for a video production.

CONCLUSION

By spending hours sitting passively in front of a TV set, children aren't engaging in activities that provide first-hand experiences or that contribute to their general academic development. Using TV listings and scripts may not compensate for the types of experiences students would have if they weren't watching TV, but they can help you (as parent or teacher) to take advantage of that time to heighten language arts and critical thinking skills. By participating in activities like the ones suggested above, students can begin changing passive viewing into active learning.

NOTES

1. Conducted by the California Assessment Program, *Television and Children* 5 (Summer 1982): 10, 12.

2. William Grant, "MASH Archievers," *San Francisco Chronicle* (21 July 1982): 1, 4.

3. Ibid.

4. Adapted from Stewart M. Hoover, "Television: Strategies for Change" in *Television Awareness Training,* p. 117.

4 Reality and Fantasy: Why Tall People Are Older than Short People

Children under the age of seven or eight view the world according to their own logic; they take things literally, even when concepts of time and space are distorted. For example, young children may believe that inanimate objects can talk and that tall people are older than short people. A child's perception of distance may be directly related to the amount of time it takes to get from one place to another. For instance, a child may perceive a city 600 miles away which can be reached by plane in 45 minutes to be closer than a city 100 miles away which takes a few hours to get to by car.[1]

After watching certain programs on television, youngsters may very well think that people can fly and cars can ride up the sides of buildings. Young children are often unable to tell the difference between TV programs and the commercials that accompany them. Older children often have difficulty separating fact from fiction in a drama. They frequently don't understand that real life is not as it appears to be on TV. And, although TV didn't create the demand for a quick and easy solution to every problem, it does reflect and reinforce the fast pace of today's lifestyles. When TV characters solve their problems quickly, children expect to be able to solve their own problems quickly, too, and become frustrated when they can't. (Even the popular TV program *Sesame Street* has been criticized. Critics claim that its fast pace and use of rapid cuts discourage concentration and give the impression that events don't need to follow logical continuity).[2]

Teenagers are likely to believe what advertisers tell them and generally fail to realize that news and documentary programs can be subjective and may present facts in a distorted manner.

Some adults confuse performers with the characters they portray, and may even trust television to the extent that they cannot accept ideas that contradict what they have seen on the tube. Even completely fictional programs, such as ones that are set in exotic places or other time periods, can be accepted as fact. (The miniseries "Shogun" was believed by many viewers to be factual. Although it was drawn from real events and people who lived in 17th-century Japan, the story was fiction.)

Docudramas usually combine fictional characters and dialogue with the portrayal of real events. It is difficult for any viewer to discriminate between what actually occurred in history and what was invented for a TV production. According to TV journalist Bill Moyers, docudramas do not accurately represent reality. He claims that:

> Docudramas cross the line between art and reality without telling you that they have done so. They are done for the sake of commerce instead of illumination, and are a very disturbing melange of fact and fantasy. Without a discriminating respect for what actually happened, they can set back the cause of public understanding by giving an illusion of what happened. They are done hastily, with little regard for the nuances and subtleties that make history intelligible. They are highly destructive of reality.[3]

In docudramas, opinions can often masquerade as facts, and viewers may believe that a producer's interpretation of an event is the correct one. As psychologist Victor Cline states:

> The very real danger of docudrama films is that people take it for granted that they're true and—unlike similar fictionalized history in movies and theater—they are seen on a medium which also presents straight news. No matter how much they call these movies "drama," they're really advocacy journalism. They can't help reflecting the point of view of the writer or the studio or the network.[4]

QUESTIONS AND ACTIVITIES

The following questions and activities are designed to promote class participation concerning what is real—and what is not real—on television.

Action-Packed Programs and TV Violence

Action!

• Young students need to develop a healthy skepticism toward the things they see on TV. Provide tapes of TV programs that show action scenes. These can include programs that feature superheroes, animated figures and inexperienced people in

Mister Rogers® Home Video: Dinosaurs and Monsters. A video production that helps children differentiate between reality and fantasy.

Photo courtesy of Family Communications, Inc. © 1979, 1986 Family Communications, Inc. All Rights Reserved.

"Standby...Lights! Camera! Action!" hosted by Leonard Nimoy takes viewers behind the scenes during the production of major motion pictures.

Photo courtesy of NICKELODEON.

positions of authority. After students have viewed the tapes, begin a question and answer session. Questions to ask your students could include the following:

How can you tell whether or not something you see on TV is real?

Can real people do what the superheroes do?

Do superheroes actually exist?

What is an animated figure? (Perhaps students can draw animated stick figures that move as pages are flipped.)

In certain cartoon and adventure shows dinosaurs are shown living side by side with people. According to what we now know based on scientific evidence, did people exist at the same time as the dinosaurs?

Sometimes on TV shows, characters that have no experience at a particular job are asked to do that job anyway. Usually, they seem to be able to pull it off without any problems. What would happen if such situations occurred in real life?

Hit Men

• Violence on TV can seem exciting to young children. This may be because the real consequences of violent acts are often not shown.

Play taped examples of violence from TV action shows for your class (e.g., shootings, fist fights, car chases). The following include some general questions that you can ask your students after they have viewed the tapes:

On many TV shows, the hero's car remains undamaged after a violent car chase. How likely would this be to happen in reality?

Who would pay for all the damage that was caused along the way?

TV heroes are often seen engaged in fist fights and brawls where people are struck by objects, such as chairs, etc. Do students believe these heroes could walk away uninjured or with minor bruises that seem to disappear within the next scene or two as they often do?

What might the real consequences be?

TV programs are often centered around criminal activity. How many programs show how the victims of these crimes may be affected emotionally?

Mistaken Identity

• Some viewers often confuse performers with their roles. Advertisers can use this to their advantage by having actors promote products so the viewer will associate the product with the actor's character and image.

Ask students if they can cite examples where this is done.

Ask students if they or someone they know has ever written to a television character (not the actor) to ask a question or tell how much they enjoy that character's particular show.

Real People

- Ask students to make five lists. They should include the topics listed here:

1. Programs that depict real events.
2. Programs with real people who talk about real events (e.g., talk show hosts).
3. Programs with actors who portray real people.
4. Programs with actors who portray realistic fictional people.
5. Programs with actors who portray unrealistic fictional people.

Students can also make a list of things animated characters do that are realistic, and a list of their unrealistic characteristics.

A Little More About Production

Passing Time

- To help students understand that events on TV shows are structured to fit the program's hour or half-hour format, have students note the elements that indicate the passing of time during a TV show. The following questions should help to get them started:

What visual and aural clues indicated that time was passing?
Did characters seem to eat breakfast and dinner within the period of a half hour?
How quickly did a scene shift from day to night?
Did characters change their clothing?
Did characters say things that indicated time had passed?
Was there a change in the weather?
Were flashbacks used?
If flashbacks were used, what techniques were used to integrate them into the program?

On Site

- If possible, arrange to have your class tour a TV studio. Students might also enjoy being part of a TV studio audience. If this can be managed and a program is selected that the class is familiar with, have students draw their impressions of what the set will look like. Questions for class discussion could include those listed below:

What are TV stage sets made of?
How many cameras are used to tape a show?
Where are the lights?
How many people are needed for a camera crew?
What happens during commercials?
What will be outside the area that is framed by the TV picture tube?

After returning from your class trip, a comparison of students' expectations and what they actually saw can be made.

Facts and Fictions: Reporting on Historic Events

● Have students write scripts for short docudramas based on historic events. For this assignment it would be best to select significant but more obscure examples from history so your students would not have preconceived ideas about what happened from novels they may have read, or movies or TV shows they may have seen. For instance, a historical docudrama could be written about the circumstances that surrounded the publication of the first newspaper in America. It was called, *Publick Occurrences, Both Foreign and Domestic,* and made its first and only appearance on September 25, 1690. The publisher's intention was to expose people who started false rumors. Authorities in Boston, however, suppressed the paper immediately.

To begin their project, students could research and discuss what life was like in 1690—what people wore and ate, their living conditions and their occupations. The circumstances surrounding the newspaper's publication and rapid demise could also be researched. With this information students could outline the action for a drama based on the steps listed below:

1. Create a possible sequence of events.
2. Create characters.
3. Plan scenes.
4. Create settings.

Students should review the script when they are finished and decide whether or not it is a dramatic and interesting representation of what happened in 1690. If students decide it is not dramatic enough, they should consider what changes might help to make it more exciting. The addition of a fictional character or a change of motivation to add conflict might add some spice to the story. The class can then discuss how, even though the drama was based upon true events, the addition of fictional characters, etc. changed the representation of what actually did happen in 1690.

● As a related assignment, students can research and collect data on an historic figure. They can develop a script based on events in that person's life.

Distribute copies of the scripts to other members of the class to read and evaluate. Questions students could ask each other include the following:

Did the events in the script actually take place?
How did the writers know what to have the characters say to each other?
What aspects were added to the scripts to make the story more interesting?

CONCLUSION

Fantasy can stimulate the imagination and encourage creativity. TV programs that star superheroes can provide an exciting escape for children as long as they realize that these characters are fictional. Adventure programs may provide "harmless" entertainment (as industry spokespeople would have us believe) but this is only if youngsters understand that dangerous actions which appear harmless on TV would have very different consequences in real life. And docudramas can provide a fascinating look at historic periods and events as long as children understand that much of what they are watching may have been invented for the program.

NOTES

1. Dorothy G. Singer, Jerome L. Singer, and Diana M. Zuckerman, *Teaching Television: How to Use TV to Your Child's Advantage* (New York: Dial Press, 1981), p. 8.

2. Marie Winn, *The Plug–In Drug: Television, Children, and the Family* (New York: Penguin Books), pp. 40–41.

3. Carol A. Emmens, "Docudramas–Revised History?" *Previews* (May 1980): 3.

4. Donna Woolfolk Cross, *Media-Speak* (New York: Mentor/New American Library, 1983), p. 227.

5 Social Issues: Not Every Father Knows Best

TV serves as a major role model and socializing influence for children, who learn by observing and imitating the activities they see going on around them. Some TV programs show people dealing with issues such as crime, poverty, old age, loneliness, death, the rights of senior citizens and the disabled, drugs and sex in a realistic manner. Other TV shows seem to encourage rule breaking and downplay moral concepts such as brotherhood and humanism in favor of greed and aggression.

On some TV programs sex may be portrayed as a dirty joke or an illicit and dangerous activity that frequently leads to trouble. In the following extract a healthy state of human sexuality is described by the American Medical Association (AMA):

> [Human sexuality] is not confined to the bedroom, the nighttime, or to any single area of the body. It is involved in what we do, but it is also what we are. It is an identification, an activity, a biological and emotional process, an outlook and expression of the self. It is an important factor in every personal relationship and in every human endeavor from business to politics.[1]

This AMA definition differs from how sexuality may be depicted on TV. The following statement is from Elizabeth Roberts of the Project on Human Sexual Development at Harvard University:

> [Television] tells the child viewer over and over that human sexuality equals sexiness and [that] sexiness is an acceptable subject if it is cloaked in humor or ridicule or viewed as a harsh, hurtful, or criminal part of life.... Affection and intimacy are viewed as inappropriate to the "real world".... hardly an integrated, rewarding, and fulfilling dimension of adult life.[2]

45

Preteens may not be able to interpret or understand many of TV's social messages. Young viewers tend to believe what TV portrays because they have no experience to compare it with and they need help dealing with frustrations that might arise when things in real life fail to work out the way they do on TV.

In a national survey that studied the effects of family problems in the classroom, 89% of the teachers responding said that societal problems were affecting their students and therefore their roles as teachers; 81% felt that a family-life curriculum that would provide opportunities for the discussion of emotions and values would be helpful.[3]

Discussion of TV programming is one way in which teachers can help students explore social issues. Research done at the Yale University Family Television Research and Consultation Center has shown that when children discuss TV programs, deep feelings are often revealed and children face issues about which they had previously been curious but which they had avoided confronting. Discussing TV shows can encourage students to clarify their own values, resist group pressure and examine sensitive issues. Often, when students face these issues in terms of characters, instead of in terms of themselves, they feel they can speak openly and avoid possible embarrassment.

A group of young people poke fun at the very issues that are most important to them on *You Can't Do that on Television,* NICKELODEON'S live format comedy show for preteens and teens.

Photo courtesy of NICKELODEON.

TV can reflect society with varying degrees of accuracy. It can provide unrealistic role models, perpetuate stereotypes and offer simplistic solutions to complex problems. On the other hand, it can encourage positive values and promote helpfulness, cooperation and self-control.[4] If students discuss the social issues encountered on TV programs they may become better prepared to deal with social concerns and could develop an increased ability to distinguish between and world of television and their own world.

QUESTIONS AND ACTIVITIES

For many social issues that concern children, there are TV programs that either confront or incorporate the topics. To facilitate discussion of each of the social issues and situations listed below, examples from current TV shows can be cited.

All in the Family

• Talk with your students about the different types of families that appear on TV. These include the traditional nuclear family, single-parent families and childless married couples. Have students list the names of characters that appear on shows depicting these different family units, perhaps singling out pre-adolescent and early adolescent characters. Below are listed some possible questions for discussion or written assignments:

> What types of homes do TV families live in? Are they always neat?
> Do values differ across income levels?
> What are the most common types of conflict in TV families? What are the most common resolutions to these conflicts?
> How do TV parents compare with students' parents?

• Have your class select a TV family they enjoy "spending time with," then ask the following questions:

> How is this family different from other TV families?
> Are the situations and characters portrayed on the show realistic?
> How do conflicts between family members develop? Are these conflicts resolved through discussion or verbal and physical abuse?
> What are the family's greatest strengths and weaknesses?
> What activities do members of the family enjoy doing together?
> Which characters do students most closely identify with?

• Now that students have some background with family units on TV, they can more easily talk about issues that concern their own families. Listed below are some ideas for class discussion:

> Describe the ideal mother.
> Describe the ideal father.
> Describe the ideal child.

How should children show affection for their parents?
How should parents show affection for their children?
What punishments do children consider to be unfair?
Why do brothers and sisters fight?
How are handicapped relatives treated by other family members?
How does divorce or separation affect children's lives?
How are conflicts resolved in students' families?
What are the problems of being a family member?
What holds families together?

Between Friends

● We all have friends, some close, some not so close. Compare friendships portrayed on various TV programs. These can include relationships between children of the same age; between older and younger people; between people of the same sex; between people of different sexes. Use the questions below to encourage class participation:

What is a friend?
How do friends on TV shows act toward each other?
What do TV friends do for each other?
Can you think of incidents where TV friends hurt one another? If so, how were the incidents resolved?
If you (the student) hurt one of your friends, how would you express your regret?

If You Really Love Me...

As discussed earlier, youngsters get a great many of their impressions about sex from what they watch on TV. Some people confuse sex with love. Others may feel that to be admired and successful they have to be "sexy."

● Older students may have confused feelings about their own sexuality. Specific episodes from TV shows can be used to discuss circumstances such as what happens to characters on TV who don't look like a "perfect 10" or what kinds of roles do attractive people play, and why do people seem to fall in love so quickly? Students could also improvise scenes based on characters such as those listed below. (If the teacher prefers, these examples can also be used as topics for written assignments or class discussion):

A young man or woman who feels that you aren't "with it" unless you are sexually active.
A young woman who feels forced to have sex with her boyfriend because he says that she doesn't really love him if she won't (or vice versa).
A teenage girl who thinks she might be pregnant.

When the scenes have been acted out, the class can discuss the consequences faced by each character in the situations.

People Helping People

• Situations often arise in which people need help. Sometimes helping another person may mean putting oneself in danger. Ask students if they have ever seen a dramatization of such an incident or perhaps a real situation that was presented on a TV news show. Once situations have been identified ask the following questions:

If students knew they would be putting themselves in danger, would they intervene to help another person?
Would it depend on who the other person was?
Can students think of any situation where they might try to stop one person from helping another?
How do students feel when they help someone else?

• Students may view other types of situations on TV in which people might want to offer help. These can include situations with handicapped people or those who are learning new skills. Sometimes it is better not to help if the person being helped may be made to feel small and helpless. The questions below can help students to think about how people can be affected in particular situations where help is offered:

When might people want to do things for themselves?
How does it feel not to be helped?
What does it mean to be a "know–it–all?"
When is it appropriate to give and receive help?

Child Abuse

• Child abuse is a topic that is receiving a great deal of attention today. Students should be able to find a TV dramatization or news report that deals with this subject.

When a particular incident has been chosen for class discussion, questions to ask your students could include those listed below:

What is the difference between discipline and mistreatment?
In the TV dramatization under discussion, who did the child talk to about the incident or incidents of child abuse? Who else could a child talk to?
Where did the child go for help in the dramatization?
Where could a child go for help in real life?

Following the Rules

● Everyone has rules to follow—in school, at home and as a member of society. Rules keep order and allow activities to progress in a relatively smooth manner.

Have students cite examples of laws and rules that must be followed. Then, discuss TV shows where some of these rules were broken. Compare what happened on the TV shows to what might happen in real life.

Responsibility

● TV programs can reflect both responsible and irresponsible behavior. To illustrate these actions, students can take examples from TV shows. They can then compare their own levels of responsibility with those of characters their own age. A discussion of responsibility could involve the following questions:

Do students think they have too many responsibilities?
Do they think they have too few?
How could they better manage the responsibilities they do have?
What types of responsibilities do they feel they could not handle?
Do students think all children of the same age should be allowed to do the same things?
How can children demonstrate to adults their readiness for responsibility?

Peer Pressure—Making the Right Choice

● Students will probably have already encountered peer pressure and may have felt forced to do something they didn't want to do because they feared they would be rejected by others. Discuss situations on TV that involved peer pressure, then have students answer the following questions:

Have your friends ever tried to pressure you into doing something you really didn't want to do? How did you respond?
What did you consider when making the decision to either go along with or not go along with the crowd?
Have you ever tried to pressure your friends into doing something that they didn't want to do? What did you do if they decided to act against your advice?
Do you think peer pressure has a mostly negative effect on people?
Can you think of any situations where peer pressure might be desirable?

● Students might enjoy acting out improvisational scenes in which peer pressure is employed. A possible scene for young students could include a youngster who is being encouraged by friends to start smoking. Older students might focus on a college student's conflict about whether or not to engage in a potentially embarrassing and harmful fraternity hazing ritual.

Discuss the scenes with the class in terms of what decisions could be made and the consequences of the actions that might be taken.

Drug and Alcohol Abuse

• Drug and alcohol use is a major social issue that may at one point or another enter your students' lives. Have students choose an incident from a TV show to discuss the following questions:

In the TV program being discussed were drugs or alcohol taken casually?
If drugs or alcohol were taken casually, were they the cause of a conflict?
Were drugs or alcohol taken to help characters relax?
Were drugs given to someone forcibly to make them do something they didn't want to do?
How did characters' behavior change when they took the drugs?
How do students think their own behavior would change if they took drugs or consumed alcohol?
Do students have one clear attitude about drugs and alcohol, or do they have mixed feelings?
What do students think of people who are drunk or high on drugs?
How might the behavior of alcoholics or people high on drugs affect their relationships with family and friends?

Discrimination

• Discrimination is a social issue often confronted on TV. Students can list instances where someone was discriminated against on a TV program—e.g., left out of a group activity or not invited to a party. The following questions can be used for class discussion or a written assignment:

How did the prejudicial attitude depicted on the TV show develop?
How might the person being discriminated against have been feeling?
Has anyone in the class ever been discriminated against?
What are the different types of discrimination?
Why do some people, communities or countries feel they are better than others?
Do *all* people, communities or countries feel superior to others?

Workout

TV can provide superficial and misleading information about careers and the labor force.

• Ask students to define what a career is, then have them answer the questions listed below:

Do people have only one career all their lives?

What kinds of skills can be transferred to a variety of jobs?
What is a "good" job?
Which jobs are worthwhile?
Which jobs would you prefer not to do?

Based on the above exercise, students can discuss jobs and aspects of jobs that are usually left out of TV programs—for instance, specific tasks and salaries.

The following questions about the jobs of TV characters should promote class discussion:

On TV, are characters ever shown carrying out the specific tasks involved in their jobs? How do students think the characters were trained for their jobs?
Are the lifestyles and manners of dress of TV characters compatible with the salaries students think they earn?
What other occupations might these characters be suited for?
How many TV characters have no discernible jobs?

• A study conducted by Linda Glennon and Richard Butsch, titled "The Devaluation of Working Class Lifestyles in Television Family Series, 1947–1977," found that while people in working class occupations constituted about 70% of the labor force, only 6% of the programs on TV featured heads of households with blue collar jobs.[5]

First, define blue collar and white collar occupations and have students research the actual number of each in the American work force. Students can then make lists of characters on TV that are engaged in blue collar and white collar occupations. A bar graph can be used to compare the actual research figures with those taken from the lists of TV characters.

To further discuss how the American work force is depicted on TV, ask students the following questions:

On TV, how many heads of households are portrayed as characters holding blue collar jobs? Are these characters shown as being as satisfied with their jobs as those in more glamorous and prestigious professions?
Which of these jobs are held by men? By women?

Wealth

• Plenty of wealthy people are portrayed on prime time TV (especially on the "soaps"). These portrayals may often be very inaccurate. Ask the following questions to find out what your students think about wealth on TV:

How are wealthy people portrayed? Do they pursue high ideals? If so, are they willing to give up their fortunes for those ideals?

Do wealthy characters ever discuss the benefits of free enterprise and entrepreneurship?

Do wealthy men and women on TV buy things of artistic or cultural value, or do they seem to buy only clothing and accessories?

How often do wealthy characters travel? Under what circumstances and for what reasons do they travel?

Do wealthy characters ever do anything to improve their intellects?

Do these characters seem to do any work for their fortunes? If they do, where did they get their job training? Are their working environments realistic?

Does being wealthy mean that you automatically can succeed at any job?

The Street Where You Live

Soap operas are one of the most common program formats that confront social issues. However, even though soap opera characters are facing real-life issues, their consequences and solutions often appear very unrealistic. For example, there are few blue collar workers, few old people struggling on fixed incomes, and no one has to worry about legal or medical bills. On TV soaps, children older than 10 months add no value to the story line unless they meet with some misfortune. Common illnesses like head colds or stomach upsets only rarely appear; if they do, they usually have a comic impact on the storyline. When illness is treated seriously, it is usually life-threatening, mysterious or unusual and ends dramatically by means of a tragic death or a miraculous cure.

● Have students write their own episodes of a soap opera and then perform them for the class. Ask the following questions:

Does anyone in the audience know people like the ones they have seen in the soap operas?

Does anyone know people like the ones in the scenes written by students?

How are students' lives similar to those of characters on soap operas? How are they different?

What types of people and situations *don't* viewers see in TV soap operas?

CONCLUSION

In real life, not all fathers are like the ones seen on TV, and not every father or mother knows best. Students' reactions to life situations are influenced by what they experience and observe and even though it appears to be a passive influence, TV *is* affecting students' behavior.

After completing the activities in this chapter students will have looked at several social issues through the "eyes" of TV, and should have a better grasp on some of the issues that affect their lives.

NOTES

1. Edwin Diamond, *Sign-Off: The Last Days of Television* (Cambridge, MA: The MIT Press, 1982), p. 43.

2. Ibid., p. 47.

3. "Family Problems: How They're Affecting Classrooms Today," *Learning 86* (1986): 36–37.

4. Glenn Alan Cheney, *Television in American Society* (New York: Franklin Watts, 1983), p. 62.

5. Meg Schwarz, ed., *TV and Teens: Experts Look at the Issues* (Reading, MA: Addison-Wesley, 1982), p. 124.

6 TV Stereotypes: What You See Is What You Get

The familiar phrase, "What you see is what you get" could be applied to stereotypes on television. Many children do not have the personal contacts or the experience to form their own opinions about groups that are often stereotyped, such as the elderly, minorities and people of different ethnic backgrounds. For many children, TV is the only source of information about people who are different from themselves.

Research conducted by Dorothy Singer, Jerome Singer and Diana Zuckerman of the Yale University Family Television Research and Consultation Center has shown that there is a relationship between the TV programs children watch and the prejudiced attitudes they express.[1] Another series of studies conducted by Melvin DeFleur and Lois DeFleur, that looked into the presentation of occupational roles on TV, found that some youngsters are more likely to trust images that are presented on TV than they are to trust knowledge gained through their own personal experience.[2]

Characters are frequently sketched in a stereotypical manner so that viewers can quickly identify and become familiar with them. If a youngster is constantly exposed to stereotypes in this way, his or her choices in terms of behavioral roles and occupations can be severely restricted. Listed below are examples of the world according to television:

- The elderly are underrepresented. Despite the fact that people over the age of 60 form a large portion of the U.S. population (and they are heavy TV viewers), they are underrepresented on TV. Only 3% of all TV characters are in the 65-and-over age group, and a disproportionate number of these are male.[3]

- On TV, men outnumber women three to one.[4] Traditionally, male characters have been depicted as being strong, smart, rational, ambitious and engaged in a wide variety of occupational roles. Traditional TV women are more passive and less achievement-oriented. Some 70% of the female characters on TV do not hold jobs outside the home (at a time when 53.1% of all American women have joined the labor force).[5] Female characters have also been depicted as being kind, unselfish and happy; their major concerns are their families, homes and appearance. Women, more often than men, are cast in light or comic roles, and are also frequently defined in status by their relationships to men. Women are depicted as being dependent on men and as gaining financial security through marriage or inheritance. Young and beautiful women are usually the main victims of violence.
- Blacks and Hispanics (and other ethnic groups) are most often cast in situation comedies, and even then only on very few shows. Characters from both groups are also more likely to be portrayed as unemployed or holding unskilled jobs.[6]
- On commercial programming that is specifically designed for children, there are even fewer minorities and females than there are on adult TV programs, and more stereotypes about them. On children's commercial programming, animals, robots and other nonhuman characters are more likely to have speaking parts than are minority characters.[7]

CHANGING STEREOTYPES

Positive minority images can be found, however, on some programs on commercial TV. Warm and happy family lives are depicted for blacks as well as for whites, children of different racial backgrounds play and learn together, and women are seen as being independent and professional people.

The Public Broadcasting Service (PBS) has consistently led the way in fostering positive role models for children's TV. Its traditional and bilingual programming presents favorable images of the disabled, portrays both male and female characters in nontraditional careers, and shows the consequences of stereotyped thinking. Unfortunately, funding for PBS projects always seems to be threatened or is actually cut. Many of the PBS programs that fostered positive role models for children were produced under the Emergency School Assistance Act, which is no longer in effect. This leaves the few programs on PBS and commercial TV that combat stereotypes pitted against the many older programs that do perpetuate stereotypes, and those that continue in syndication.

While some stereotypes appear to have been weakened, other new ones are emerging. It seems that every woman is now expected to be a "superwoman" who manages to bring home the bacon while effortlessly handling a marriage and a family at the same time. It would appear that woman's new goal is to achieve success by pursuing money and power. At least the glamorous and strong-minded female characters who are in lead roles in a number of TV shows exhibit these qualities. And television advertising often utilizes the image of the competent, successful, liberated woman to promote a wide variety of products.

It's questionable, for the moment, whether programs that represent positive role models can counteract the greater number of stereotypes that are perpetuated through traditional programming. FCC statistics do indicate that there has been some improvement within the television industry in the number of women and minorities employed behind the scenes. In 1982, women in broadcast TV made up 34.7% of all employees, and minorities held 16.9% of all jobs.[8] A closer look at the makeup of the TV labor force, however, reveals that women and minorities are rarely employed where it counts. This includes positions that have an effect on station policy, such as promotion managers and research directors. Few minority employees or women work on a regular basis as TV writers, and the industry is not benefiting from the input these people could bring to program content.[9]

QUESTIONS AND ACTIVITIES

The following questions and activities will help students to become more aware of the ways in which TV stereotypes people (including themselves). They will also look at some of the reasons why stereotypes appear so frequently on TV, and how they can combat them.

White Hats, Black Hats

Stereotypes permit us to label people too conveniently and consequently make judgments about other people or groups of people too easily. One definition states that "stereotypes are based not on an inductive collection of data, but on hearsay, rumor, and anecdotes—in short, on evidence which is insufficient to justify the generalization."[10]

Discuss stereotyping with your students and how it differs from making generalizations. Note that people may assume that things they read or see on TV are true even though they have not experienced them in real life.

• To help students identify any stereotypes they might relate to, ask them to make lists of adjectives and phrases that describe males and females. Compare these descriptions to those in Figure 6.1.

• Ask students to act as program directors for TV. Have them describe the types of characters they would select for certain parts. The following questions could be used to facilitate this exercise:

If students were going to cast "good guys" versus "bad guys," how would these characters look?
How would they dress? Talk? Act?

Figure 6.1: Areas That Distinguish Traditional Sex-Role Behaviors

1. **Aggression.** Boys are often encouraged to be aggressive. They are more likely to gain approval when they engage in rough play and fighting and are often involved in violent and antisocial behavior. Girls are encouraged to be more passive.

2. **Activity.** Boys like to play outside. They are encouraged to be more active than girls, and find it more difficult to sit still.

3. **Curiosity.** Boys are expected to be curious—to explore and to find out how things work. Girls are usually not interested.

4. **Impulsiveness.** Boys are expected to be impulsive and take chances. They have trouble resisting temptation and can be easily distracted. Girls tend to take fewer chances and are more able to resist temptation.

5. **Anxiety.** Females are more fearful and anxious than males. Anxiety is demonstrated by compliant and obedient behavior, and by showing more interest in doing the right thing.

6. **Importance of Social Relationships.** Females are encouraged to be nurturant from an early age. They are encouraged to show interest in babies and play with dolls. In general, females are expected to display more empathy and show more cooperation in social relationships than males are.

7. **Self-Image.** Males are taught to view themselves as being powerful, with control over events that take place in their lives.

8. **Achievement-Related Behavior.** Males are expected to set higher levels of aspiration for themselves than are females, who often feel less confident and often doubt their abilities.

Source: Adapted from *Images of Life on Children's Television: Sex-Roles, Minorities, and Families,* by F. Earle Barcus. Copyright 1983 © Praeger Publishers. Reprinted and adapted with permission of Praeger Publishers.

If students were going to cast a family, what would members of the family be like? Would they be physically attractive? Would there be grandparents? If so, what would the grandparents be like?

Would any of the members of the family be handicapped? (How many TV families include handicapped people?)

What do students think of when they picture blacks, Jews, Hispanics and Asians? If students were writing roles for these people, what types of jobs would they have? What kind of educational background? Where would they live?

Based on the questions, students could try a "reality check" to see if their impressions are accurate. For example, if they don't belong to one of the ethnic groups listed above but have friends who do, they can see the ways in which they may match these stereotypes and the ways in which they differ.

• Discuss the exaggerated characteristics of people that contribute to the creation of stereotypes. These include behavior, styles of dress, manners of speech, facial expressions, gestures, etc. Then, list and describe the various stereotypes found on TV. Use the following list of exaggerated stereotypes as an example:

dumb blonde
helpless young woman
senile old woman
buxom mama
domineering mother
macho male
stubborn old man
swarthy bandit
computer whiz
tempermental artist
effeminate hairdresser
pitiable handicapped person
smart person with glasses

Ask students if they think TV creates these stereotypes or just reflects or reinforces them. Also discuss the role humor can play in either diminishing or reinforcing stereotypes.

TV Images

• Ask students to describe the characteristics of different types of people portrayed on TV. Have them support their views by providing examples from familiar TV programs. The list below can be used as a sample:[11]

smart person	aunt
blind person	uncle
deaf person	bigot
drug abuser	musician
farmer	lawyer
athlete	criminal
poet	doctor
secretary	scholar
law-abider	librarian
judge	tourist
politician	flight attendant
cowboy	disabled person
rich person	reporter
detective	middle class family
scientist	lower class family
enemy	single person
banker	dropout
teacher	astronaut
housewife	psychic

When the first part of this activity has been completed, initiate a class discussion based on the following questions:[12]

Do the characters on the TV programs that students use to describe the different "types" of people correspond with students' personal experiences?

Which groups are represented most accurately on TV?

Which groups are represented most inaccurately?

Is there any group which might like the way that it is portrayed on TV?

If students belonged to a group that was portrayed inaccurately on TV, what could they do about it?

• Discuss with students why minorities and the elderly may be misrepresented on TV. The following questions can be used as a part of class discussion:

Are the TV networks racist? If you think they are, do you think they are consciously so? Is it because advertisers might feel that their products won't sell to minority groups?

Commercial broadcasters claim that they can't cater to special interest groups because they have to serve too broad an audience; do students think this is so and that people are interested in seeing programs that reflect only their own age groups and interests?

Viewer's Logs

Students can use viewing logs to analyze how male and female characters and minorities are depicted on sitcoms, dramas and children's programs. (See Figures 6.2 and 6.3.) Logs can help students to organize information, answer questions, focus on specific issues and form their own conclusions.

• To get a variety of samplings, assign different TV programs to different students at the beginning of a week. Some students can log the characteristics of

Figure 6.2: Viewing Log: Character Stereotypes

Program _____

Channel _____ Time _____

Type of program _____

Character_____ Male _____ Female _____

Approx. age_____ Race _____ Occupation _____

Marital status _____ Physical characteristics _____

Description of personality _____

Major activities (e.g., chasing criminals, washing shirts, etc.)_____

Places where usually seen _____

Method of problem solving (e.g., violence, discussion, lets someone else decide, makes own rational decision, etc.) _____

Figure 6.3: Log for Determining Sex Role Stereotyping in Occupations Portrayed on Television

For the week of _____

Occupational role	Male	Female
Professional/technical (e.g., entertainers, athletes, media personnel, scientists, engineers, airplane pilots, doctors, social workers, lawyers, judges, clergy, teachers)		
Managerial (e.g., royalty, political leaders, police chiefs or commissioners, military officers, businesspeople, managers, directors, owners of businesses, ships' captains, principals/ headmasters, heads of organizations)		
Sales people		
Clerical workers		
Craftspeople (e.g., skilled artisans)		
Transportation equipment operators (e.g., truck or taxi drivers, toll collectors)		
Nontransport operatives (e.g., sailors, ship crew members)		
Farmers and farm laborers		
Nonfarm laborers		
Service workers (e.g., janitors, cooks, "busboys," exterminators, barbers, tour guides, police officers, detectives, park rangers, sheriffs, night watchmen)		
Household workers (e.g., servants, babysitters)		
Students		
Homemakers		
Retired persons		
Illegal occupations		
Employed, but occupation uncertain		
Not shown as employed		

Source: F. Earle Barcus, *Images of Life on Children's Television: Sex-Roles, Minorities, and Families* (New York: Praeger, 1983), pp. 42–47.

male characters, others can log those of female characters. At the end of the week, use the logs to find out if stereotypes such as those mentioned in some of the above assignments appear in the newer programs. The logs can also be used to answer the questions listed below:

How often are children under the age of 16 featured on TV?

Do students think children their age are accurately depicted?

Do students think adults decide what children should be like based on what they see children doing on TV?

How many working women are portrayed?

How many of these working women are mothers? (Note: Nearly 50% of American mothers today are working outside the home. In five years 75% of U.S. mothers are expected to be working outside the home.[13])

Are men identified as being single or married as often as women?

Are female characters usually younger than male characters?

How many female characters are depicted as being independent?

How many only *appear* to be independent (e.g., they are always saved by their male companions)?

Are successful women always depicted as being glamorous?

Are any new female TV stereotypes emerging such as the wealthy, manipulative matriarch?

How do males and females achieve their goals? Through charm? Deceit? Violence? Persuasion? Cruelty?

Are the sexes portrayed similarly on adult and children's programs? (Note: According to a 1982 study commissioned by Action for Children's Television, commercial children's television presents a smaller percentage of female and minority characters than prime-time television. When minorities and women do appear, they are generally negatively stereotyped.) [14]

How are laborers in manual or production jobs portrayed on TV? Are they most often portrayed as caricatures? Are they ever portrayed as being bigots with closed minds and little education?

How often do viewers see people of Chinese, Japanese, Italian, German, Polish or Jewish descent portrayed on TV?

When such people are portrayed do they usually have a characteristic accent?

Are people from ethnic groups more likely than white people to be victims of crimes? Are they more likely to be portrayed as criminals?

What roles are minorities usually seen in (e.g., servant, sidekick, transient)?

How many current network programs feature elderly people as being capable and intelligent individuals?

Do handicapped people always have things done for them? Are they portrayed as being happy? Are they portrayed as being equal to their peers? Do their lives seem to revolve around their problems?

Although there are millions of physically or mentally handicapped people in the United States, how often are they featured on dramatic, news, sports and variety programs? When they are featured, do students think they are being featured in an accurate way?

What would happen if the lead role in a popular series was played by a handicapped person?

In the Minority

Currently, a number of TV programs include characters belonging to nonwhite minority groups. These minority portrayals, however, may not always be positive. For example, children's cartoon comedy shows may contain the most blatant ethnic stereotypes.[15] Brenda Grayson, a critical writer on children's television, has the following to say about the portrayal of blacks on TV:

> An older sophisticated viewer might question this world in which black females and males are constantly shown expressing hostility toward one another, but to the young, unsophisticated child viewer, this is life as it is in "the real world." Studies have suggested that young children see a series of separate and fragmentary incidents rather than the story of a television film. Thus, while the overall theme and story line of a program might be of social significance and redeeming moral value, young viewers may be tuning in only to the seemingly comic aspects of these abusive verbal attacks. Moreover, as many parents can attest, young children are excellent mimics of what they see on the television screen. Such examples are hardly inspiring. For black children, the total effect of these negative images accumulating day after day is teaching self-hate and resulting in destructive self images. For white viewers, such depictions reinforce common misconceptions about how blacks behave.[16]

• After discussing the different minority groups, have students research and report on the following questions:

Name current shows that include characters who belong to minority groups. What type of program do the majority of these characters appear in? Are the characters providing positive role models? For every negative role model these characters portray can a positive one be found?

How many programs include characters who portray a strong, intelligent minority father figure?

In comedy programs where minorities are featured, do hackneyed displays of affection seem to "soften" verbal attacks and make them seem alright? What might minorities be learning about themselves from viewing such comedy programs?

Which nonwhite minority is most visible on TV today? Is this minority shown in a variety of program formats and lifestyles? Is this minority portrayed as participating in all levels of the social, political, economic and cultural aspects of society? What are viewers learning about minorities and how they should be treated?

Critical Acclaim

• Now that students have a better idea of how stereotypes are formed, they can write "letters of recommendation" (or create awards and present them) to producers of TV programs they feel meet the following goals:

1. Encouragement and reinforcement in all children of a positive regard for themselves that grows out of an understanding and pride in their own unique cultural heritage, experience and environment.
2. Provision for minority children of heroic and successful peer and role models who exemplify, convey and put into practice the best features and attributes of a moral and just world.
3. Portrayals for children of the positive aspects that the rich diversity of cultural pluralism brings into American society.
4. Demonstration and encouragement of intercultural communication, cooperation and friendship.[17]

CONCLUSION

Students have now confronted many of the stereotyped attitudes they may have had about different groups of people. This should help them to handle more easily the many encounters they will have with people throughout their lives.

The following chapter (Chapter 7) further discusses TV's role in the development of children's attitudes toward the world with an examination of commercial advertising on TV and how children relate to it.

NOTES

1. Dorothy G. Singer, Jerome L. Singer and Diana Zuckerman, *Teaching Television* (New York: The Dial Press, 1981),p. 125.
2. Aida Barrera and Frederick P. Close, "Minority Role Models: Hispanics," in *TV and Teens,* edited by Meg Schwartz p. 92.
3. Bradley, S. Greenberg, *Life on Television,* cited in *Fighting TV Stereotypes: An ACT Handbook* (Newtonville, MA: Action for Children's Television, 1983).
4. National Institute of Mental Health, *Television and Behavior,* cited in ACT handbook, 1983.
5. Ibid.
6. Ibid.
7. F. Earle Barcus, *Representations of Life on Children's Television,* cited in ACT handbook, 1983.
8. *Fighting TV Stereotypes: An ACT Handbook* (Newtonville, MA: Action for Children's Television, 1983).
9. Ibid.
10. Barcus, *Images of Life on Children's Television: Sex-Roles, Minorities, and Families* (New York: Praeger, 1983), pp.70–71.

11. Adapted from Rosemary Lee Potter, *New Season: The Positive Use of Commercial Television with Children* (Columbus, OH: Charles E. Merrill, 1976), pp. 30-31.

12. Ibid.

13. Joan Hanauer, "TV," *San Francisco Chronicle,* 16 March 1985.

14. Peggy Charren and Cynthia Alperowicz, "Talking Back to the Tube," *Family Learning* (1984): 7.

15. Barcus, *Images of Life on Children's Television,* p. 115.

16. Brenda Grayson, "Minorities on TV," In *Television Awareness Training: the Viewer's Guide for Family and Community,* edited by Ben Logan (New York: Media Action Research Center, 1979), p. 141.

17. These goals were used in the development of the "Righteous Apples" television series. Topper Carew, "Minority Role Models: A Case Study, 'The Righteous Apples'," in Schwarz, *TV and Teens: Experts Look at the Issues* (Reading, MA: Addison-Wesley, 1982), pp. 107-108.

7 Messages from Our Sponsors

We are all influenced by advertising. If you've ever bought an article of clothing because it had a designer label, or a cleanser with a tag that claimed it was a "new and improved" product (but it performed just like the old one), or a cosmetic item that was advertised as being able to make you more youthful or attractive, then your purchase was influenced by what the product was "telling" you. According to manufacturers, products "speak" to consumers, and products have plenty to say. They promise everything from health and popularity to a successful new image. Advertising also provides consumers with information about new items and can be helpful in the selection of products.

If it is difficult for adults to sort out all the messages that are delivered by product advertising, then it must be even more difficult for youngsters, who have no understanding of how advertising can inform, persuade and even manipulate them. If an animated figure on the TV screen tells a child that a particular box of cereal is "GRRRRRREAT!" then to the child, it must be so. A breakfast food commercial may prominently feature an athlete leaping over high hurdles. A child who identifies with the athlete may believe that by eating this particular breakfast food, he or she will become as strong and agile as the athlete.

Another TV commercial may feature smiling parents with their children seated around a breakfast table. Children may think that by buying and eating this cereal they will be able to get their parents' approval and affection. Older children might be attracted to phrases such as "pure and natural" or "homemade flavor" with little knowledge of what these phrases actually mean. They may also believe that a particular cereal is "part of a balanced breakfast" without realizing that most of the nutrients required to make a balanced meal are provided by the addition of other food products. (One study conducted by the University of Georgia in the late 1960s showed that if children ripped up their cardboard cereal boxes and just ate them, they'd be getting as much nutrition as they would from the cereal itself.)[1]

Ads for toys can be equally misleading. If a TV commercial shows a group of children playing together with a toy, a young viewer can interpret the ad as saying: "If you own this toy you'll be popular and will make friends too." A toy such as a model space station may appear to be larger than it actually is because of its placement in relationship to other objects or people in an ad. If the model is further enhanced by being illustrated in a fantastic setting (such as floating in space and shooting laser beams at alien space ships), a child may take the image literally and expect the toy to perform all the functions shown. Unless it is clearly stated in an ad that particular parts of a toy are sold separately, that batteries are extra or that assembly is required, a child will probably expect everything portrayed on the ad to be inside the box and ready for use when the toy is purchased.

Children typically view some 400 ads on TV each week—ads that can change their attitudes as well as the ways in which they play and eat. For example, there are more ads for sugar food products than there are for other types of food. It's therefore no surprise that the consumption of soft drinks, pies, cookies, desserts and snacks by children has risen dramatically over recent years while the consumption of more healthful foods, such as milk or fresh fruit, has declined.[2] By their own admission, children are influenced by commercials in areas other than nutrition, and a variety of surveys and experimental studies dating, back to the 1970s have confirmed this. For example, studies conducted as part of the 1972 *Surgeon General's Report* demonstrated that children who regularly watched TV asked for the foods, toys, games and many adult items they saw advertised.[3] Studies conducted by both the Council on Children, Media and Merchandising and the National Science Foundation (NSF), indicate that children respond to over-the-counter drug ads by forming certain opinions toward the use of medicine. One NSF study revealed that children with heavy exposure to medical advertising worried more about getting sick and were more likely to "feel better" after taking medicine.[4]

Young children are especially vulnerable to the influence of TV commercials because they are unaware of the sophisticated persuasive techniques that are used in commercial advertising. According to the Council on Children, Media and Merchandising, just the fact that something is viewed on a TV screen gives it an aura of acceptability and importance. When children see an item promoted on the screen, they think it *must* be good, otherwise it would not be there in the first place.[5]

Children are influenced not only by commercials on TV, but also by ads in stores that use TV characters to promote products. Character licensing (the practice of leasing character names or identities to businesses that want to capitalize on their success) has long been a popular way for toy manufacturers to profit from familiar children's TV programming. Now, however, the opposite has also come true and characters originally associated with product advertising are being featured in series and prime-time children's TV specials. TV programs that were inspired by toys blur the relationship between TV programming and advertising. It seems that children's programs can become protracted commercials for toys—a practice that can deprive children of diverse and creative programming and which is not consistent with the responsibility of the "public trust" that has been given to commercial broadcasters.

If students can learn to analyze the commercials they see on TV, they will be better equipped to evaluate the claims that advertisers make; they will be able to look beyond the sell and become less likely victims of deception; and they will learn to separate the double-talk from the facts.

QUESTIONS AND ACTIVITIES

Test Pattern

The commercial potential of TV was recognized from the start as advertisers realized that TV could have a dramatic affect on consumers.

- Use the questions listed below to discuss the impact of commercials on TV.

What is the purpose of advertising on commercial TV?

Have you ever been introduced to a new product through a television advertisement?

In what ways, other than TV commercials, do you learn about new products or services?

How many types of TV advertisements can you name? (Examples include commercials that pay for the airing of scheduled programs; political ads that are paid for by political candidates; network promotions that are paid for by the networks; and public service advertisements that are given free air time.)

Do you think TV commercials can be misleading?

Have you ever purchased an item just because you liked the advertisement that promoted it on TV? What was it about the ad that made you want to buy the product? At the time you purchased the product, was it something you really needed? Did you enjoy the product?

Have you ever purchased a product that you saw advertised on TV which turned out to be a disappointment when you got it home and tried to use it?

If you are currently thinking of buying a product that you've seen advertised on TV, how much do you actually know about the product? How much of this information was provided to you by the advertisement?

Why do you buy particular brands?

Have you ever bought a brand name out of loyalty to a company?

Has an advertisement ever made you feel that if your purchased a generic or "no-name" item you would be purchasing an inferior product?

Have you ever had a conflict with your parents because they wouldn't buy you something that you saw advertised on TV?

On TV commercials, people often seem to be very excited about doing their housework. Do you know anyone who gets as excited about this as the people on TV do?

Would you miss TV commercials if they were banished from the airwaves?

Deception and Detection

• Deceptive advertising is often difficult to define and detect. In one case, a soldier sued the U.S. Army for false advertising because he felt there was a great deal of discrepancy between the promises made by Army advertisements and the reality of military life. The government claimed that the soldier was ridiculously "naive" to have taken such ads seriously; it claimed that he should have known that the promises made were "puffery" and "simply braggings on the part of the government." The government's defense made sense to the federal judge hearing the case, who ruled in favor of the U.S. government.[6]

Based on the above example, ask your students questions such as those listed below:

Do students agree with the judge's ruling?

In TV commercials, are things that should and shouldn't be taken seriously always made obvious?

• Product advertisements make many claims. Discuss with your students claims found in TV commercials such as those listed below:

A manufacturer of aspirin claims that tests for quality proved that its aspirin was superior to other brands. The commercial, however, does not explain why the aspirin is superior. (The test may have only proven that this particular brand of aspirin is whiter than other brands.)

A manufacturer of a product that induces drowsiness states that its product can ensure a good night's sleep. The ad, however, does not indicate that there are other things that will also induce drowsiness.

Another ad may describe the "complete toothpaste." The wording here suggests that the toothpaste the consumer is currently using is missing something. The ad, however, never explains what that something is.

• Ask your students how they would react in each of the following situations:

A consumer group discovers that the "wholesome and natural" granola that students saw advertised on TV and subsequently purchased and ate for lunch (just because they thought it was wholesome and nutritious), is actually filled with preservatives.

The Federal Trade Commission declares that a mouthwash which is advertised on TV as being an effective remover of plaque when it is used as part of a regular program of dental care and hygiene, won't do anything when it is used by itself.

After reading the labels on several competing products, students discover that several of them are produced by the same manufacturer.

Students discover that their favorite ice cream with the foreign-sounding name is actually manufactured locally.

● Advertisers are required to comply with certain broadcast regulations—for example, celebrities cannot openly endorse products on commercials directed toward children. Advertisers can get around this, however, by leading viewers to "see" endorsements that aren't there. By settings the scene for a cold medicine commercial in front of a medical building advertisers imply that the product is safe and scientifically approved; an ad for encyclopedias that is set in front of a school implies that the books have been approved as educational aids.

Ask students to create advertisements for products they find around the classroom, giving the impression that professional organizations are endorsing them.

● Some TV advertisements use misleading words or phrases to describe products, e.g., phrases that sound scientific. Others hedge claims by saying that "mileage will vary," while others make a product sound indispensable without really telling the viewer what the product does. Ask students to point out examples of such advertising techniques.

What's Fair?

A number of studies have shown that, over time, children begin to distrust the accuracy of commercial messages even though they still believe much of what they see and hear on TV. About 40% of the 9- to 12-year-olds in one study believed that the products advertised on TV were often "not like the ads say," although this skepticism may be limited to things the children had had experience with. Researchers also found that 10- to 13-year-old children generally accept the messages for pain relievers, personal hygiene and other health-related products as being true.[7]

● Some critics say that it is unfair to advertise to young children, especially those under the age of eight, because they don't understand what commercials are intended for and can't separate them from scheduled programming.

Discuss with your older students whether or not they think they understood TV commercials when they were younger.

● Use the following questions as topics for class debate:

Should all ads directed toward children be taken off the air?

Should TV broadcasters be required to insert electronic signals at the beginning and end of all commercial children's ads to activate devices like the Children's

Advertising Detector Signal that would block the commercial? (The FCC has been petitioned for approval of such a device that would be bought by parents who wanted to automatically tune out commercials at home.)

Would devices such as these infringe upon the advertiser's First Amendment rights or constitute government interference in the content of children's advertising?

Is it an unfair financial or technical burden for broadcasters to provide an electronic signal that activates such a device? (Coded signals are already used to coordinate the timing of programs and commercials.)

Would these devices fall within the FCC's public interest responsibility (i.e., to see to it that the public interest isn't dominated by commercial interests)?

Viewing Logs

After discussing common techniques of persuasion used by advertisers (see Figure 7.1) have students keep viewing logs of the commercials they see on TV. (See Figure 7.2.) Have students use the following list as a guide when they complete their logs:

1. The target audience is the group that an advertisement is aimed at. It can usually be identified through observation of the ages and occupations of the characters, the setting, the persuasive techniques used, and by analysis of the promises made in the ad.
2. Voice-over is usually a voice that comes from offstage. It can be male or female and the message can be sung or spoken. Sometimes the voice has a foreign accent.
3. The pace helps to create a particular mood or image. It can be fast, slow or moderate.
4. The format can be documentary, demonstration, animation, mini-drama or a scene taken by a hidden camera.
5. The tone of a commercial is indicated by whether there is a hard or soft sell.
6. Casting describes the characters in the ad.
7. Technical tricks include holding a product close to the camera without any people or other objects around so the product appears to be larger than it actually is. Unusual lighting, color or sound effects, rapid cuts, slow motion and animation are also often used.
8. Other tricks that advertisers use are the inclusion of additional items or accessories that don't automatically come with a product; the use of appealing and/or useful packaging such as a keepsake container or a souvenir tin; and the offer of a premium.

• Using the information obtained in the viewing logs, have students answer the questions listed below:

Do commercials appear at the same time in all half-hour programs? In all hour programs?

Figure 7.1: Common Advertising Techniques

Persuasive Methods

Testimonial. A famous person endorses a product.

Plain Folks. The consumer is made to feel that he or she has something in common with the people in an ad, who are just like "every day" people.

Bandwagon. Everybody else is doing it, so if the viewer wants to be popular and socially acceptable, he or she will do it, too.

Sex Symbols. Attractive models are used to promote a product so consumers will believe that by purchasing the product, they will be attractive, too.

Fear. The consumer is made to feel insecure or unprotected, and is shamed into buying a particular product.

Self-Evident Truth. Advertisers present their opinions so they sound like universally accepted facts.

Transference. To transfer an idea or emotion that makes people feel good, to a particular product so they will identify that product with that "good feeling."

Snob Appeal. Advertisements directed toward the consumer's desire for status.

Name Calling. To judge the competition without providing evidence.

Slogans. Short phrases to help the consumer remember a product.

Buzz Words. Popular words with a positive association used to describe a product.

Loaded Words. Words with an emotional appeal.

Card Stacking. Deception through simplification, half-truths, or information that is no longer appropriate.

Repetition. Repeating a word or phrase so the consumer is certain to notice and remember it.

Facts and Figures. Statistics that are presented without interpretation, yet are used to prove a point or provide "evidence."

Time and Money Savers. Appeals to the consumer's desire to save time and money.

Direct Order. Appeals to the belief that people need and respond to authority ("Buy it now!").

Figure 7.2: Viewing Log for TV Commercials

COMMERCIALS LOG

TV Channel _____

Program _____ Air time _____

Air time of commercial _____

Length of commercial _____

Product being advertised _____

Target audience _____

Setting _____

Voice over _____ Male _____ Female _____

Pace _____

_____

Persuasive techniques _____

_____

_____

Format _____

Technical tricks _____

_____

Tone _____

Casting _____

_____

Other techniques _____

How many commercials are there in half-hour and hour programs?

What is the estimated amount of time viewers spend watching commercials during an evening of TV viewing? Estimate the amount of time for a week, a month, a year.

Are there more commercials in children's half-hour programs than there are in prime-time programs? Are there less? Is the number of commercials the same?

How often do girls appear in commercials for "action" toys? (Advertisers have discovered that young boys do not respond well to ads with girls promoting toys.)[8]

What do advertisements for toys and games that are aimed at girls generally emphasize? (Those aimed at girls usually emphasize beauty and popularity. Those aimed at boys generally emphasize power, noise and speed.)[9]

Are there more boys than girls in commercials for candy, cereals and drinks?

How many organizations have students seen advertised through public service announcements? Which groups advertise most often?

In what ways are public service announcements similar to commercials?

What special techniques are used in public service announcements to motivate people?

Trick or Treat

The following list of questions is suggested by the Children's Advertising Review Unit, National Advertising Division, Council of Better Business Bureaus, for use as guidelines when viewing children's advertising:

- If assembly of a product is required, does the ad say so?
- Is a child or adult shown doing something unsafe?
- Does the ad suggest that children will be superior to friends or more popular if they own a particular product?
- Does the ad suggest that an adult who buys a product for a child is better or more caring than one who does not?
- Does the ad employ any demeaning or derogatory social stereotypes?
- In ads featuring premiums, is the premium offer clearly secondary?
- Is there anything misleading about the product's benefits?[10]

Students can look for examples of each of these points in children's advertising, and can develop a guide of their own for use at home (with parents).

New! Improved! Bigger! Better!

In addition to persuasive techniques and tricks, advertisers use other methods to promote both familiar and new products.

• Advertisers often take familiar products and create new interest in them by developing a "selling hook" (e.g., some ads refer to cars as "impressive" or "ultimate driving machines"). Have students write their own selling hooks for familiar products.

• Another way in which manufacturers create interest in products is by developing a consumer need where one doesn't exist. To demonstrate this, students can create new needs by starting a group such as a humorous "Department of Disease Development" where ailments (irregular fingernail spots or unsightly elbow wrinkles) are invented. Student members of this new "department" can write advertising copy that they think will convince other students that they have these new ailments and problems or are likely to develop them soon. (Visuals can be used to make their arguments seem more convincing.) When students have effectively established that such imaginary problems exist, they can then try to sell products to help alleviate them.

• If a manufacturer desires to have an established product promoted to increase sales, new packaging is often the answer. New product packages can be designed in unusual shapes with attention-getting graphics, or they can project specific images that consumers will want to identify with. (It is interesting to note that in its broadest sense, "package" refers not only to a parcel but to an idea where the package and product become so closely associated that they cannot be separated.)

Students might be interested in creating their own new packaging for products they are familiar with. These could include products packaged in sturdier containers, space-saving individual packages or packages that are easier to carry. Hold a contest for the best new package created by a student.

Target Practice

When writing product advertising, the age of the consumer group that is to be targeted is given a great deal of consideration. The five age categories that are generally "targeted" in demographic analysis include ages 2 to 11, 12 to 17, 18 to 34, 35 to 55, and 55 plus. Prime-time TV programs and their accompanying commercials are created primarily to attract members of the 18 to 34 and 35 to 55 age groups. Although members of the 35 to 55 age group tend to have the most disposable income, those in the 18 to 34 group spend more money. Younger adults, presumably building their households, make more purchases of expensive "hard goods" (refrigerators, microwave ovens, automobiles, and so on).[11] The geographic areas in which consumers live are also given consideration by advertisers. You would not, for example, expect to sell many snowblowers in Southern California.

• Students can rewrite advertisements they have seen on TV and target them for different segments of the population and different geographic locations. The following list of questions could serve as a guideline:

What approach would students use to sell a diet cola product to men over the age of 40? to Eskimos? Californians? inner city youth?

Would a hot, humid setting help to sell ice cream in Hawaii?

Would a cartoon figure help to sell a toy to children?

Would a celebrity endorsement of a pair of jeans be a selling point for teenagers? What celebrities?

You Are What You Eat

Nearly 60% of all child-oriented commercials sell food products that conflict with guidelines established by the Senate Select Committee on Nutrition and Human Needs.[12]

• To illustrate this statement have students list all the foods advertised on TV on a given Saturday morning. Students can present these lists to the class. Use the questions below as part of class discussion:

Are the four basic food groups represented?

Can children create a balanced diet with the foods that are represented?

Do the advertisements for these foods talk about nutrition?

Are unhealthful or valueless foods portrayed as being nutritious?

What attitudes or habits about food might young children develop as a result of constant exposure to these ads?

• To enable students to understand how TV ads promote the use of alcoholic beverages, discuss the implications of slogans that make alcoholic beverages appear as rewards or indicators of social status. Use the following questions as a part of your class discussion:

What do slogans tell people about the use of alcoholic beverages? (Students can rewrite certain slogans so they discourage the use of alcoholic beverages.)

Do alcoholic beverages (at least according to the advertisements) appear to be essential for a happy, successful and socially fulfilling life?

According to the ads, how often should people "reward" themselves with beer or wine?

• A Washington DC-based coalition called "Project SMART" (Stop Marketing Alcohol on Radio and Television) wants to ban advertisements for alcoholic beverages on broadcast media. If that is not possible, "Project SMART" wants warnings to accompany these ads. Ask students to respond to the questions listed below:

Would students support such a campaign?

What warnings and statistics concerning alcohol abuse by teenagers would students use if they became involved in such a campaign? (Students could begin their research by contacting Alcoholics Anonymous, a local alcoholism information center, or hospital alcoholism/drug treatment programs listed in the phone book.)

Would students consider this campaign, as liquor industry leaders do, to be "neo-prohibitionist"?

Are the implications made in advertisements for beer the same as those in advertisements for wine?

Do students think warnings would help to reduce liquor consumption?

If not, what other approaches might be taken?

What were the effects of banning cigarette ads from television?

Are fewer people smoking cigarettes as a result?

Self-Promotion

Despite the fact that it costs thousands of dollars to run a commercial on TV, the cost to the advertiser amounts to only a few dollars for every thousand viewers who see the ad. This is a much less expensive way of getting a message across to more people than it would be to send a written advertisement to each of these same people through the mail. For this reason large corporations often use TV as a medium to promote themselves and counter criticisms that might be leveled against them.

Students can form groups that represent large companies, public utilities or specialized associations. They can then create advertising copy that serves their group's best interests. When writing their copy students should consider what types of information should and should not be included in their ads. Listed below are some examples of tactics taken by advertisers:

- An ad sponsored by a power utility that was intended to favor the building of a nuclear power plant could show a family living happily with inexpensive energy. On the other hand this ad would probably ignore the safety issues involved with radioactive waste and hazardous conditions such as nuclear accidents.
- A car manufacturer might sponsor a public service advertisement for air pollution control.
- A company that contributes to the creation of acid rain might sponsor a promotional ad for clean water.
- A sponsor could present its cause as being everyone's cause and suggest that none of "us" want government intervention when it is the sponsor who wants to avoid government regulation.
- Sponsors will also be concerned with the TV program material during which its commercial will be shown. A sponsor would not want a villain to be shown using its product, for example.

CONCLUSION

After completion of the above exercises, students should be more aware of how commercial advertising on TV has affected their attitudes toward the items they buy. With the ability to analyze commercials (even if it is just to ask whether or not a toy does all the things it is shown doing on TV), children are one step beyond the sell and less likely victims of deception.

NOTES

1. Donna Woolfolk Cross, *Media-Speak: How Television Makes Up Your Mind* (New York: Mentor/New American Library, 1983), p. 17.

2. Kate Moody, *Growing Up On Television* (New York: McGraw-Hill, 1980), pp. 101–102.

3. Maurine Doerken, *Classroom Combat: Teaching and Television* (Englewood Cliffs, NJ: Educational Technology Publications, 1983), p. 98.

4. Ibid., p. 112.

5. Ibid., p. 100.

6. Cross, *Media-Speak,* p. 15.

7. Diane E. Liebert, "Television Advertising and Values," in Logan, *Television Awareness Training,* pp. 46–47.

8. Doerken, *Classroom Combat,* p. 98.

9. Ibid.

10. Dorothy G. Singer, Jerome L. Singer and Diana Zuckerman, *Teaching Television: How to Use TV to Your Child's Advantage* (New York: The Dial Press, 1981), pp. 170–71.

11. David Marc, "Understanding Television," *The Atlantic* (Aug. 1984): 37.

12. Peggy Charren and Cynthia Alperowicz, "Talking Back to the Tube," p. 7.

8 Video Violence: The Dark Side of the Tube

A growing number of educators, social scientists and mental health professionals are beginning to believe that the violence portrayed on commercial TV may have a harmful effect on the nation's youngsters. And no wonder: the National Coalition on Television Violence estimates that the average American child watches 24,000 shootings on TV by the time he or she reaches the age of 15.[1] The Coalition also reports that violent acts on TV—those viewed by adults as well as by children—increased by 65% from 1980 to 1984.[2] One survey that measured the amount of violence found on TV indicated that an average of eight violent acts per hour could be seen on prime-time television in 1982. Another study, conducted in 1983, observed that children as young as the age of four watched an average of 8,000 violent acts a year on TV cartoon shows.[3]

TV producers need simple, action-packed stories that will hold viewers' attention. Nowadays, stories about crime and violence seem to fit the bill the best. Violence has long been used by writers to give dramatic impact to the consequences of brutality, and to broaden readers' minds to the understanding of the human condition. The violence on TV, however, is sometimes *only* violence which is portrayed without a context, explanation or background.

Acts of violence on commercial TV can also be distorted. For example, one third of all TV characters either fight or commit crimes; almost 85% of the gun shots that are fired miss their mark, giving the impression that guns can be less dangerous than they actually are;[4] and 3 out of every 10 senior citizens on TV are likely to be beaten or robbed when the real-life figure for attacks on the elderly is less than 1%.[5]

TV has become a place where crimes occur about 10 times more often than they do in the real world, and criminal heroes and the police can break the law (in the name of justice) even though constitutional rights may be ignored.[6] Children who watch all this violence can gain a distorted and innaccurate view of life. Research has indicated that adults—and possibly children—who watch heavy doses of TV violence tend to exaggerate the extent and seriousness of crime in America and see the world as being more dangerous than do people who watch less TV.[7]

In 1982, the National Institute of Mental Health (NIMH) published a 10-year update of the 1972 Surgeon General's Report, *Television and Social Behavior.* The new report, titled, *Television and Behavior: Ten Years of Scientific Progress and Implications for the Eighties,* reached the following conclusions:[8]

1. TV is a powerful teacher.
2. There is increasing evidence that there is a cause-and-effect relationship between viewing violence on TV and subsequent violent social behavior.
3. The effects of TV viewing on children can be modified through active intervention, supervision and guidance of children by their parents.

The report concluded that there was "overwhelming" evidence that excessive violence on TV causes violent behavior in children who watch TV, and that this violent behavior is manifested through aggressive play and the acceptance of force as a solution to problems.[9] These NIMH conclusions were echoed later in 1985 when the American Psychological Association maintained that "viewing televised violence may lead to increases in aggressive attitudes, values and behavior, particularly in children."[10]

Research conducted by Albert Bandura, a noted leader in the study of TV violence and its impact on the behavior of children, has found that children take in new responses simply by watching others and that these responses can last over an extended period of time. Bandura's numerous experiments show that children who watch aggressive adult models on TV later perform twice as aggressively as those who do not watch such models.[11] Comments made by parents, outside the "laboratory," tend to support these results. The consensus is that children who view large numbers of violent TV programs at home seem to exhibit a greater degree of physical and verbal aggression than those who don't. They imitate violent acts and repeat violent phrases. They may even model themselves after superheroes (typically involved in violent situations) rather than characters who portray more traditional roles such as doctors or firemen.

Both teenagers and adults have been involved in crimes that are similar to incidents they had previously seen acted out on TV. In 1973, two separate groups of youths, one in Boston, MA, the other in Miami, FL, re-enacted a scene from a TV movie by setting a woman on fire. During that same year, a 17-year-old admitted to having re-enacted a murder he had seen committed in a TV production.[12] More recently, in 1984, a Milwaukee man set fire to his estranged wife the day after the broadcast of a made-for-TV movie about a battered wife who had killed her husband by setting fire to his bed while he slept.[13]

While most of the evidence indicates that violence on TV has a negative affect on many young viewers, some researchers argue that by watching aggressive scenes, viewers may be able to purge feelings of fear and anger thereby reducing subsequent violent behavior. For example, children who grow up in punitive and restrictive households can use televised violence to relieve the anger they cannot discharge directly at their families. Proponents of this "catharsis theory" claim that televised violence satisfies some emotional needs by reducing drive and arousal and thereby relieves frustration and aggression. This theory is based on the premise that people can always separate fantasy from reality—an assumption that cannot be made for all young children and, as evidenced by the number of violent acts inspired by TV, not true for some adults as well. (The theory also fails to take into account the premise that learning occurs through observation, repetition and imitation.) These same researchers go on to say that many of the studies that criticize TV violence are methodologically flawed, statistically slight and perhaps colored by the investigators' intellectual bias against the medium. Other researchers point out that the 20-year rise in the crime rate that began in approximately 1960 was not caused by TV, but rather by demographics—i.e., the post World War II "baby boomers" who came of age in the early 1960s. Teenagers and young men account for a large share of the crime committed in the United States. With the baby boom generation now entering middle age, statistics show that the nationwide crime rate is beginning to decline.[14]

Studies may never prove beyond the shadow of a doubt that there is a connection between viewing violence on TV and aggressive behavior. Researchers do not claim that TV is the only, or even the primary cause of violence and aggression in our society. The extent to which a person responds to televised violence is influenced by a number of factors including education, moral training and family experience. Children *do,* however, see acts of violence on TV that are used to resolve conflicts (even though physical confrontations are suppressed in real life), and these acts of violence appear plausible and normal because they are acted out in realistic settings with realistic people. And, by portraying life as ceaselessly violent, TV continues to show people in the worst possible way.

QUESTIONS AND ACTIVITIES

Reflections on Video Violence

• Have older students discuss their impressions of violence in real life based on their viewing of TV violence. Ask the following questions:

Do students think that criminal and violent acts are often rewarded or made to appear attractive on TV?

Do students think that bitter and ruthless conflicts between persons or groups on TV are portrayed as being the ordinary state of affairs?

Do students feel that TV violence that takes place in unfamiliar settings such as in westerns and science fiction productions, is as believable as violence set in familiar and realistic settings?

Do students feel that they are capable of violence? If so, under what circumstances?

Pow! Bam! Zap!

The antics of certain time-honored cartoon characters are considered too violent by some critics. In an April, 1984 article in *The New York Times,* the National Coalition on Television Violence was reported to have said that even some cartoons on the Walt Disney cable television channel contain acts too violent for viewing by children. It claimed that these programs are almost as violent as Saturday morning cartoon shows on the commercial television networks. Research conducted by the Coalition found that an average of 19.3 violent acts are committed per hour in Disney cartoons with an average of 9.1 violent acts an hour in Disney's non-cartoon programming. (However, according to Disney officials, the network has been endorsed by the Parent Teachers Association and the National Education Association.)[15]

• Have students analyze violence in cartoons by asking them to watch programs at home. Taped examples can also be used for viewing in class. Class discussion could include questions such as the following:

Is violence used as the major means to keep the action in the cartoon going?
If the program producers removed all the casual violence in the cartoons, would there be a story?

You've Got It, I Want It

• Have two students go to the front of the class to act out an improvisational scene. The theme of this scene is that one student has something the other student wants. (The desired item could be a book, a food item, etc.) The first student should then try to obtain the desired item from the second student by any means other than physical force or theft.

Have the class evaluate the scene by discussing methods that can be used to solve conflicts. Such methods include:

negotiation
mediation (use of an intermediary such as an impartial person or a jury)
persuasion
co-optation (getting the opposition to change sides)
coalition (joining sides with the opposition)
bargaining (buying, trading)
withdrawal (running away from or ignoring the conflict)

• As a further assignment, have students listen to newscasts and read news periodicals to find ways in which people deal with conflicts (war, terrorism, strikes, protests, etc.). Then have them list the methods they have found in order from the most physically aggressive to the most socially acceptable.

Finding Alternatives

• Discuss with students specific scenes from TV shows that resulted in violent activity. Then have students reenact a modified version of the scene with a nonviolent ending. If new characters had to be developed to make the scene less violent, ask students why the original characters' personalities were not well-rounded enough to allow them to act in a nonviolent manner.

Sticks and Stones

Aggression doesn't have to take the form of physical violence. Aggression can also be verbal (i.e., insults, put downs, name calling), and it appears on some TV programs.

• Have students list TV programs in which they find large amounts of verbal aggression. Then, have them discuss why verbal aggression may seem funny or exciting. Incorporate into this discussion students' feelings about verbal aggression and how they would react if someone made fun of them in real life.

Silent Crimes

Crimes not often portrayed on TV are the "silent" or "white collar crimes," such as tax evasion or illegal waste disposal. Media critic Robert Cirino states that "Even though the violence and death caused by individual crime affects thousands, it is on a smaller scale than the silent and unseen violence inflicted on Americans by the illegal disposal of poisonous pollutants, poor auto safety design, uninspected meat, contaminated food, overuse of pesticides, misleading advertisements and violations of work-safety standards."[16]

• Ask students why they think such "silent crimes" are not popular topics for TV programming. Then have them look through news periodicals for examples of such crimes. These can be used as topics for crime programs students might like to write and then act out.

Poor Reception

• Have students form a "Standards of Decency Department" that would be responsible for rating TV programs based on the amount of violence they contain. Members of the department should develop a TV violence rating code (the motion picture code could be used as a model). Logs such as the one in Figure 8.1 can be used to tally the number of violent acts in episodes from a variety of series.

Assign different channels to different groups of students to see which channel has the most violent programs per evening and per week. Students might also want

Figure 8.1: Viewing Log: TV Violence

Program _____
Day_____Time _____
Channel _____

(List each act separately.)

	(1)	(2)	(3)
Type of violent or aggressive act (Fist fight, car chase or crash, bombing or other explosion, arson, foot chase, murder, kidnap, rape, suicide, brawl, theft, burglary, blackmail, other)	_____	_____	_____
Reason for violent or aggressive act	_____	_____	_____
Victim(s)			
Perpetrator(s)	_____	_____	_____
Result of act	_____	_____	_____
Could the conflict have been resolved without violence?	(Yes)___ (No)___	(Yes)___ (No)___	(Yes)___ (No)___
If so, how?	_____	_____	_____

to invent and name their own "violence award" which could be sent, along with a critical letter, to the producers of the winning TV show or program manager of the offending station.

Courting Violence

The societal effects of TV violence have been heard in a few US court cases. In one incident, a 15-year-old boy killed an elderly woman in Florida. His family tried to sue the major networks on the basis of "involuntary television intoxication," claiming that the boy had imitated negative behavior he had seen depicted on TV. The US District Court in southern Florida dismissed the motion because no specific television program had been cited.[17] Prior to this incident, a nine-year-old girl had been sexually assaulted in California by four youths. The girl's lawyer claimed that the youths had been influenced by a TV movie that was aired on one of the networks three days before the incident occurred. The case was subsequently dismissed on grounds that the station's right to broadcast was protected by the First Amendment and that there had been no intention to incite violence. The network station claimed that the program cited was a serious drama about the problems that can take place in a girls' reformatory.[18]

• Put TV on trial. Have students write a scenario for an incident similar to those mentioned above. Students can invent a situation in which a violent crime was committed that imitated a TV movie that was aired on a make-believe network. Several students can defend the producers of the movie against legal action that might be taken by victims who claim that the perpetrators of the crime were influenced by the movie and that the network is therefore guilty of criminal negligence. The perpetrators themselves might try to accuse the network of wrong-doing by claiming that they are not guilty due to insanity based on the influence of prolonged TV viewing. Students should research actual studies and cases to develop their arguments for or against the responsibility and therefore the guilt of the TV network.

• Questions to ask your class about TV and programming responsibility could include the following:

Do students feel parents should be held accountable for allowing their children to watch too much TV?

Should a TV network be held responsible for violent acts that may take place after the airing of a violent TV program if the program was not very realistic?

If one makes the assumption that violence on TV leads to more violence in the world, should one also assume that love stories lead to more love in the world and comedies to more humor?

Considering the age of viewers, should programs containing violence be broadcast during certain time slots, such as long after the family hour?

Should the amount of violence on TV be limited only on children's shows?

Should all TV violence be censored?

CONCLUSION

One definition of violence calls it "the overt expression of physical force against others or self, or compelling action against one's will on pain of being hurt or killed or actually hurting or killing."[19] One need only view TV for one evening to see that there are several shows that reflect this definition in their main themes. To curb such violent programming is considered by some to be an infringement of free speech and freedom of expression. In general, the courts have found form and content inseparable with regard to First Amendment protection. Film and television drama is protected speech, and freedom of expression remains.[20]

It is difficult to distinguish between First Amendment rights and what TV producers should be responsible for, since the behavior of people is usually studied within the context of an artificial experiment, abnormal in time frame and setting. It is, therefore, also difficult to judge how people might act in everyday situations and to establish a clear cause/effect relationship between what they watch and what they do. Students, however, may be able to evaluate their own behavior based on data they have collected on their TV viewing habits. By looking at this research and the activities of their peers, students can gain a better understanding of how televised violence affects them and the way they perceive the real world.

NOTES

1. Bob Greene, "Television, the Violent Intruder," *San Francisco Examiner,* 27 January 1985, "This World," p. 5.

2. Geoffrey Tooth, "Why Children's TV Turns Off So Many Parents," *U.S. News and World Report* (Feb. 18, 1985).

3. Greene, "Television, the Violent Intruder," p. 5.

4. Peggy Charren and Martin W. Sandler, *Changing Channels: Living (Sensibly) With Television* (Reading, MA: Addison-Wesley, 1983), p. 63.

5. Ibid., p. 48.

6. Ibid., pp. 61–63.

7. Based on Glenn Alan Cheney, *Television in American Society* (New York: Franklin Watts, 1983), p. 48 and Eli A. Rubenstein, "Television and the Young Viewer" *Television Awareness Training,* p. 65.

8. John Burns, "Whither Children's Television? " *Telemedium,* March-June 1984, p. 2.

9. Glenn Alan Cheney, *Television in American Society* (New York: Franklin Watts, 1983), p. 48.

10. *Chronicle of Higher Education,* (13 March 1985): p. 5.

11. Maureen Doerken, *Classroom Combat: Teaching and Television* (Englewood Cliffs, NJ: Educational Technology Publications, 1983), p. 38.

12. Doerken, *Classroom Combat,* p. 68.

13. "Footnotes" column, *The Chronicle of Higher Education* (Oct. 17, 1984).

14. Ibid.

15. "Disney TV Called Violent," *The New York Times* (24 April 1984).

16. Donna Woolfolk Cross, *Media-Speak: How Television Makes Up Your Mind* (New York: Mentor/New American Library, 1982),p. 113.

17. Dorothy G. Singer, Jerome L. Singer and Diana Zuckerman, *Teaching Television: How to Use TV to Your Child's Advantage* (New York: The Dial Press, 1981), p. 175.

18. Ibid., p. 175-176.

19. Gerbner's definition. "Television and the Young Viewer," by Eli A. Rubenstein, *Television Awareness Training,* p. 64.

20. George Comstock, "Juvenile Crime," in *TV and Teens: Experts Look at the Issues* (Reading, MA: Addison-Wesley, 1983), p. 187.

9 News and Politics: Get Me the Man in the Elephant Hat

TV is the primary source of news for the average American. It is also the most trusted. Much of the news we see on TV, however, has not been selected because of its political relevance, educational value or broad social purpose, but for its audience appeal. Producers of news programs sometimes talk about how a "show" worked or moved—not about the news it contained, and they refer to the time actually devoted to the news (averaging only 8 to 12 minutes per half hour) as the news "hole."[1] TV news show directors are constantly engaged in a struggle between the purpose of journalism and the need for TV news programs to be profitable—between accurate and perceptive reporting and show business.

NEWSROOM PRIORITIES

Instant coverage, or news right off the satellite, has become a newsroom priority. Never mind that live reporting may not add to the viewer's understanding of what is happening—the technology and its ability to provide "raw reality" have become more important. Some TV stations may even try to give viewers the impression that an event is being covered while it is still happening by reporting from the scene where the event took place much earlier.

Time restrictions also receive priority attention. They limit the amount of coverage that is given to certain stories and determine when and if others will appear. Often the concern about time causes reporters to cover "pseudo events" (events created for the convenience of the reporter), so there will be something to air in a given time slot. Time considerations can also cause reporters to rush a story which may result in limited research and therefore less coverage of a particular news item. An example of this would be a news reporter who, in a rush to get a story "in," interviews those people who are readily available rather than those who are informed. The result is that news stories become primarily headlines since there is little time to gather, investigate, research, provide background for and interpret the news.

Decisions of the Media Personnel

Before a newscast is aired decisions have to be made by media personnel to determine which stories should be neglected, which should be emphasized and which should be shaped and grouped together. Media personnel have a great deal of control over the types of opposition views that will be aired, and newscasters may choose to air groups that are in accord with their own views. (Prominent groups are more likely to be selected, while groups with nonconventional views are not.) News personnel also speculate on the possible consequences of news stories, whether private affairs can be made public and whether newspeople are generating political actions or events through their investigations—a problem that became especially relevant with the rise in urban riots and unrest during the 1960s, when suggestions were made that TV was causing the very disturbances it was reporting.

In his book, *Sign Off: The Last Days of Television,* Edwin Diamond explains that TV, "by the presence of its cameras, lights and crews, inspires or intensifies disturbances—an assertion based, in large part, on the further assertion that individuals and groups who seek to publicize their viewpoints will, sometimes, perform for cameras and microphones."[2] This view is certainly supported by the increasing number of terrorist hostage situations that have erupted around the world since the late 1970s, in which terrorist hijackers or kidnappers seem to need the attention of the media to get their political opinions disseminated.

Analyzing the News

The activities in this chapter are intended to encourage students to explore the factors that determine what is—and is not—news. They examine the relationship between news and politics, and the principles on which the free press and constitutional liberties are built.

When analyzing the news, students should be encouraged to relate events to their lives as much as possible. Events that have occurred in other parts of the country or world can become more interesting to students when they understand how these events may affect them at home.

QUESTIONS AND ACTIVITIES

The Early News

• Communication has many functions in society (either primitive or modern). A few are listed:[3]

1. Communication helps people to find out what is happening in their environment so they can be aware of opportunity and danger.
2. Communication helps individuals or groups determine how to respond, or perhaps not respond to what is happening in the outside world.
3. Communication helps each new generation learn from the previous generation how to get along in the world.
4. Communication provides a vehicle for entertainment and amusement within a group.

Students can explore the dynamics of communication on a primitive level by imagining that they belong to a primitive tribe. Use the four descriptions listed above to answer these questions:

What types of events would members of this primitive tribe want to report?
How might these reports affect future activities of the tribe?
How would the primitive reporter's role differ from that of the tribal story teller?
Does the safety of individuals within the tribe depend in any way on accurate reporting of particular events?
Would the functions and guidelines used by tribal reporters be appropriate for modern reporters?

News Is . . . .

• The following is a list of definitions for "news" as it is described in a modern sense. Have students write their own definitions of "news," then compare these with the interpretations listed below.

1. News is knowing about and relating events that are of interest to at least one other person.
2. News is information people receive second hand about the world; events and processes that are not available to them through their immediate personal experience.
3. News is what interests people or what people want to or perhaps ought to know. It can be an unusual event that may have happened, or an event that will happen and is going to affect many people.
4. News is what the reporter or news editor says it is.
5. News is an attempt to make sense of one day's history.

Codes of Ethics

Journalists have certain responsibilities concerning the accuracy and relevance of what they report as "news." The following extract is part of the Television Code of the National Association of Broadcasters:

> Television is seen and heard in nearly every American home. . . . Television broadcasters . . . are obligated to bring their positive responsibility for pro-

fessionalism and seasoned judgment to bear on all those involved in the development, production and selection of programs...television programs should not only reflect the influence of culture, but also expose the dynamics of social change which bear upon our lives. ... Television broadcasters and their staffs occupy positions of unique responsibility in their community's needs and characteristics in order to better serve the welfare of its citizens ... a television station's news schedule should be adequate and well balanced. News reporting should be factual, fair and without bias... Good taste should prevail in the selection and handling of news: Morbid, sensational or alarming details not essential to the factual report, especially in connection with stories of crime or sex, should be avoided. News should be telecast in such a manner as to avoid panic and unnecessary alarm.[4]

• A rule widely followed by media personnel is that when information is disclosed it must be in the public interest and not do excessive harm. Explore this issue with students and whether or not the media should have unrestricted access to information. Use the following questions:

What types of news items do students think should be broadcast (i.e., should plans on how to manufacture a bomb be shown on the evening news)?

Should the media be excluded from having access to secret or sensitive, but important information? To prisons? To crime and accident sites where the general public is excluded? To all public events?

If students think the news should be censored, who do they think should do the censoring?

• Divide the class into teams to debate the following:

How far should news reports go before they have entered too far into the private affairs of people? Should the criteria for this be the same for people in the "public eye" as for private citizens? (Older students might want to support their views with the results of court rulings concerning citizens' right to privacy and the activities of the media when reporting on the personal affairs of people whose lives have become a matter of public interest.)

Does a person who agrees to a televised interview forfeit his or her right to privacy?

How does the "gag rule" (e.g., prohibiting the coverage of cases that involve official corruption) help to assure a fair trial? What are its adverse affects?

• As a written assignment have students create an imaginary society in which the press is unable to gather information and disseminate it freely. Students could include their thoughts on how the lack of a free press would affect them as students, and what the results might be if information about governmental activities was kept from the press.

Students can also study the role of the media in authoritarian and nonauthoritarian regimes and write about how such regimes would use the media to maintain their power.

Trials and Tribulations

In a 1981 decision, the Supreme Court ruled that state courtroom broadcasts did not violate a defendant's Sixth Amendment right to a fair trial. Forty states now permit at least partial televised coverage of certain cases. Some states (e.g., New Jersey and Connecticut) have expanded television access to trials. Only thirteen states give the defendant in a criminal case veto power over cameras in the courtroom. The remaining majority leave the decision up to the judge. Where TV coverage is permitted, it is usually under the same conditions that apply to newspapers and other publications.

The debate continues with the networks and local stations trying to persuade the Federal courts to relax *their* ban on cameras in the courtroom. Lawyers and judges claim that cameras add nothing to fact-finding (at least one judge, however, has said that TV "keeps you from getting as easily misquoted").[5]

It has also been noted that children can be more confident when they see defendants on TV. When a California nursery school operator and six employees were arraigned on charges of sexually abusing 18 pupils, the court proceedings were televised. The deputy district attorney prosecuting the case was quoted as saying, "The children saw the defendants in court and in custody. . . . It was very reassuring to them."[6]

This issue was further highlighted by a cable channel's live coverage of a trial of six men accused of raping a woman on the pool table of a New Bedford, MA, bar. A 12-year-old boy in Rhode Island who had seen the televised trials later sexually assaulted a 10-year-old neighbor on his family's pool table. This incident caused many people to wonder about the influence TV has on people's perceptions of reality and fantasy. The controversy continues, however, and as one TV producer has claimed, since trials are going to be covered anyway, live coverage would be preferable because the audience could hear the defendant's testimony for themselves rather than having to rely on a reporter's version.

- Ask students what they think about this issue. Use the following questions:

Do students think the public should view live coverage of court trials on their TV? Why? or Why not?
Do students think there is a possibility that televising trials could infringe upon a defendant's right to a fair trial?
Do students think that defendants should have the right to decide whether or not they want cameras in the courtroom when their cases are tried? Should the judge make the decision? What about the plaintiff in the case?

Politics and the Newsroom

TV news programs present information to large audiences at one time which gives them the potential to influence a great number of people. Politicians are aware of this and have become concerned about the way they appear to millions of viewers during political broadcasts. For this reason, most political candidates now have media advisors to help them create positive images. These media advisors work primarily with political advertising. Paid political advertisements are placed in TV schedules in spots designed to attract specific audiences and in "news adjacency" spots—slots within or near the early evening newscasts and in news magazine shows. One result of this type of placement is that even though they are not actual news items political ads can often be confused as such by viewers.

Making an Impression

Political advertisements address audiences in several basic ways. Four are listed below:[7]

Biographical spots identify a politician's personality and highlight his or her career. This is done through the use of quick cuts (e.g., the politician's "Huck Finn" childhood; training at Annapolis; work with minorities).
Content or **aura spots** focus on a candidate's idealogy. These spots allow a candidate to avoid confrontations with specific issues by creating an impression (e.g., that of youth and vigor or strong character).
Endorsement commercials highlight people who support a particular candidate.
Dramatic attacks criticize an opponent's presumed faults.

Some typical styles of presentation in political advertisements include the following:[8]

cinema verité, jostling cameras and quick cuts
omniscient narrator, a camera looking in on an unstaged event or conversation
one-on-one, the candidate's sincere sell

● During an election year students can easily observe the many types of political ads that appear on broadcast television. Discuss students' reactions to these ads. Ask the following questions:

Do students think political advertising spots help candidates to win votes?
Do students think these spots can be confused with news items?
Can students identify any techniques used in political ads that are similar to commercials used to sell products?

Casting Votes

The potential political effects of the press were realized and anticipated as much as 40 years ago when the following list of categories was developed:[9]

1. Activation, the arousal of public interest and encouragement of voters to seek out information about candidates and issues.
2. Reinforcement, the reinforcement of existing political beliefs along with the bolstering against change.
3. Conversion, campaign propoganda that can convert voters from one candidate or party to another.

• Ask students whether or not they think political news reported through the media serves to reinforce the status quo or to alter it. Older students may have voted, others will have to ask their parents. Include the following questions:

Did media coverage of a particular campaign cause students (or their parents) to change their original opinion about a candidate? Did it help them to make a choice when they were undecided? Or, did they look for stories presented by the media that were consistent with their own political views?

Do students think the networks should project winners of major political contests before the polls actually close?

Would students still go out and vote if a winner had already been declared?

All the News that Fits

A half-hour newscast, minus commercials, is actually 22 minutes long. A typical broadcast consists of 6 or 7 taped "hard news" stories, each being 1 or 2 minutes in duration. One or two slightly longer feature stories or continuing special reports may be interspersed with the hard news. The verbal reports or "tells" last about 15 to 30 seconds each. These introduce and punctuate taped stories and summarize those that do not lend themselves to visualization or in-depth coverage.[10] Students can summarize this information for themselves by using viewing logs. (See Figure 9.1.)

• Based on the information gathered in the viewing logs, ask the following questions:

On a typical half-hour news broadcast, how much time is devoted to the news? To sports? To weather? To an in-depth story or special feature? To reviews, commentary or consumer spots?

What are the corresponding figures for an hour-long newscast?

Students can also take notes on what devices were used to make the news appear more exciting. Such devices can include maps, charts, live reports, stock footage, photographs, interviews, taped/filmed segments and creative camera techniques.

• Have students compare a news story on TV to the coverage the same story was given in a daily newspaper. (It has often been said that the text of a half-hour

Figure 9.1: Viewing Log: News

Channel _____ Local _____ Network _____

Time _____

Story _____

      Length _____

      International _____ National _____ Local _____

      Feature _____ Sports _____ Weather _____ Business/Finance _____

         Arts _____ Human Interest _____ Other _____

Story _____

      Length _____

      International _____ National _____ Local _____

      Feature _____ Sports _____ Weather _____ Business/Finance _____

         Arts _____ Human Interest _____ Other _____

Story _____

      Length _____

      International _____ National _____ Local _____

      Feature _____ Sports _____ Weather _____ Business/Finance _____

         Arts _____ Human Interest _____ Other _____

Devices used during the newscast _____

_____

_____

Advertisements

      Location in program _____

_____

      Length _____

newscast would fill two columns of the front page of certain newspapers.) Ask the following questions:

Does seeing a newscast on TV have the same impact as reading about the same news item in a newspaper?

Did the video portion of the newscast add anything to the report?

Based on the newspaper report, was anything in the telecast misleading?

How does the TV news language compare with the language, style and story-telling techniques used in the newspaper report?

Ask students the following questions to compare the order of stories in newscasts with those in newspapers:

Are the same stories or same *types* of stories considered important?

What order do stories, sports and weather generally follow on newscasts? In the newspaper?

Do international, local and human interest stories appear in the same places in in the newspaper each day?

Telling Stories

Ideally, TV news stories should include the following three elements:

1. Lead, an opening line that serves as a "narrative hook" to arouse the audience's curiosity. These should be written in the present tense so stories appear to be coming "hot off the press."
2. Drama, a conflict that will keep the viewer watching.
3. Snapper closer, a closing that provides a sense of resolution (preferably an optimistic one).

Teasers concerning upcoming stories should be placed before commercials so viewers will return when the commercials are over. These can include phrases such as "Coming up: the perfect 10" (which actually refers to an athlete's performance). News stories should also be grouped together thematically (e.g., presidential news should be grouped together, as should be foreign, political and economic news).

Newsbreaks also announce upcoming stories. These often appear in the prime-time hours between the early and late evening newscasts and typically consist of two or more items that are wrapped around a 10-second commercial. Their content is generally hype rather than information and may consist of nothing more than headlines or teasers.

• Ask students to select recent news stories that were covered on TV. They should write brief descriptions of the stories indicating the source (e.g., newscast, documentary, news magazine or interview) and a discussion of the probable reasons why the story was included in the program (see Figure 9.2). Students can also discuss whether people will be affected by the story on a local, national or international level as well as the techniques used to tell the story, such as visuals, interviews or expert opinions.

Have students discuss whether the stories aired were "newsworthy," and whether the placement of a story either earlier or later in the program tended to emphasize or minimize its importance. Students can also note examples of geographical bias. (Do most stories concern only their local area?)

• Ask students to write their own news stories based on items they have seen on TV or read about in the newspaper. They should incorporate the three suggested

Figure 9.2: Some Criteria for News Selection

Economic pressure may be a primary consideration in news selection. Since most production costs are covered solely by advertising income, offerings must appeal to large numbers of potential customers for products to sell. Programs and news stories must be directed toward prime consumption audiences (the general public or specialized audiences).

High impact news items (those that are relevant to viewers' lives) can make a story newsworthy.

Hard news (major crimes or disasters) usually has priority over **soft news** (interviews and in-depth reports).

Familiar situations about which people are concerned or situations that pertain to well-known people or events (political figures and celebrities) often make the news.

Geographical proximity, or stories that are close to home are of particular interest to viewers—it is believed by some, however, that this emphasis on news close to home could cause neglect toward news concerning foreign people and customs which could leave Americans deficient in their understanding of international affairs.

Timely and **novel** news is exciting news and can overshadow news that may be of more lasting significance. Social issues may also be ignored unless a dramatic event takes place (e.g., inhumane conditions are discovered in a nursing home).

elements listed above (lead, drama and snapper closer) in their stories. As a further assignment, students can write teasers for their stories and select news items that should be grouped together. (If your school has video equipment, you may want to have students produce their own newscast based on events that can be covered in their community.)

Bad News/Good News

• Ask students to cite examples of hype, commercialism, sensationalistic news reporting and sensationalistic teases (that are broadcast during newsbreaks and usually followed by minimal coverage providing little information or analysis). Students can also compile a list of recent stories that were inflated far beyond their importance (i.e. a rock concert tour or a presidential sneeze).

On the other hand some news stories such as those that involve investigative reporting can cause action that results in a toxic waste cleanup or investigation of political corruption.

These students are producing their own news program by covering a street festival that took place in their community.

Photo courtesy of Jack Herman

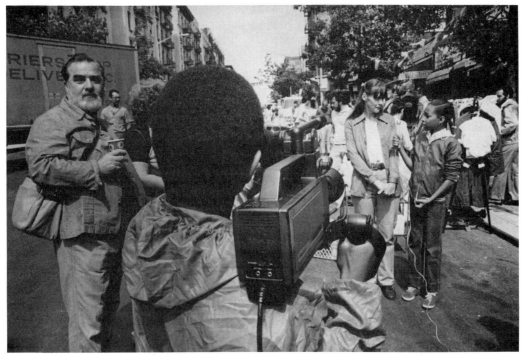

Photo courtesy of Jack Herman

News Formats

There are several basic newsroom formats (see Figure 9.3). One format, the "happy news" style of reporting, best illustrates the conflict that arises between presenting news as information and presenting news as entertainment. This style of newscasting gives the listener what he or she wants and leaves out real information in favor of getting higher ratings. (The high point of news as entertainment was probably reached by a station in Fort Myers, FL, that used a dialing-for-dollars technique to hook its audience. During the show, the news director randomly selected viewer phone numbers from a fishbowl. If the owners of the numbers were watching and called the station during the broadcast they won money.)[11]

• Have students write their own "happy newscasts" that present current events in as positive and entertaining a manner as possible. Stories should be upbeat, reported in language that soothes and pacifies and end on a happy note to keep the viewer from becoming too upset.

After the newscast has been given in class, ask students if they learned anything from the report.

Figure 9.3: Basic TV News Formats

Formal. The anchor, weathercaster and sportscaster sit in front of a camera and read the news. There is no conversation among-on-air personalities or off-the-cuff comments.

Eyewitness. "We are there" newscasting during which reporters deliver the news live and on location whenever possible. This type of report was made possible by the use of mini-cams that allow reports to be broadcast directly from the field.

In the newsroom. The "busy newsroom" effect created by cluttered desks, clicking machines, ringing phones and people rushing about. This scene is often used as a teaser for the late-night newscast, and is often staged.

Informal. On-air news people become personalities who exchange comments and humor. The weathercaster is often the most frequent target of humor in this format.

Happy talk. The emphasis is on humor, jokes between personalities, upbeat stories and weathercasters with funny props.

Tabloid. This style resembles an on-the-air gossip magazine. Emphasis is on blood, sex and deviance, miracle cures and strange occurrences.

Source: Adapted from Leonard Sellars, "How Television Sells the News," *San Francisco* Magazine (Nov. 1981) pp. 72–73.

Students can also keep records of the number of "good news" (i.e., positive, personal interest) stories that appear during a week on the network news programs. Ask students the following questions:

How many "good news" stories appear on a typical newscast?
Do students find these stories entertaining? Interesting? Boring?
Do "good news" stories make students feel good?

Profiles and Talking Heads

There are five general types of news programs: newscasts, news magazines that include profiles and in-depth looks at various subjects, interview programs, documentaries and live special-event coverage that can range from sports coverage to a presidential speech.

TV news magazines usually combine two types of reports. These include stories that are intended to act as a social force, and which usually uncover corruption, and human interest features or soft news. Although there isn't a prescribed length for each segment, TV magazines try to reach a balance by maintaining pace and variety.

• As a viewing assignment, have students watch a TV magazine program or documentary. Ask the following questions:

Do students feel too much time was devoted to any particular segment of the program?
How did the organization of segments on the magazine show compare to those on newscasts?
Were investigative pieces objective or did they lead the viewer to a predetermined conclusion?
Do students feel they tended to side with the reporter and assumed that his or her point of view was correct?

• Use TV listings (or call a local TV station) to obtain the list of guests who will be appearing on a particular interview program (sometimes referred to as "talking heads" because there is little visual interest). Have students research and compile background information on each of the guests (one group of students can research each guest). Students can then write questions they would like to ask each guest if they had the opportunity.

Before students watch the program, discuss why the guests may have been selected, their backgrounds, issues they are involved with and how they might or might not affect a community. After watching the program, compare students' questions with those asked by the journalists. Use the following questions:

Did journalists ask the same types of questions as those posed by students?
Did interviewers try to elicit direct answers to their questions?
Did the guests or subjects circumvent any questions while sounding as if the questions had actually been answered?

Were interviewers and subjects well informed?

Did interviewers ask new questions based on the subjects' answers?

Were the subjects interrogated or did journalists allow for an exchange of ideas?

Were interviews structured?

Did questions asked during each of the interviews cover a variety of topics, or was one subject explored in depth?

Students can also compile a list of people in the news they would like to see interviewed. Check the TV listings to see if any of them are scheduled. Also try to find instances where topics discussed on an interview program are reported on the evening news or in print—especially where contrasting views are expressed.

Making the News

As was discussed earlier, TV news coverage has, at times, been blamed for causing some of the news it reports by encouraging people to stage events for TV audiences. Discuss with students whether or not they feel this is true. Students can draft their own guidelines for responsible, objective reporting of political and violent events on TV. These can be compared to production standards developed by the networks (see Figure 9.4). Students can also refer back to these network standards

Figure 9.4: Production Standards for Reporting Disturbances

- Be restrained, neutral, and noncommittal in your comments and behavior despite the verbal and/or physical abuse to which you may be subjected by the participants.
- Cover the disturbance *exactly* as it happens with no staging whatsoever; make no request or suggestion of any kind which will, in *any* way, influence the participants to do or refrain from doing *anything.*
- Report the disturbance soberly, factually and unemotionally.
- Avoid coverage of (1) self-designated "leaders" if they appear to represent only themselves or (2) any individuals or groups who are clearly "performing."
- Do not describe a disturbance as a "riot" unless the police or some other responsible agency or official so designates it. Do not call a disturbance "racial" until it is officially so described.
- Avoid reports about "crowd gathering" following incidents involving police in known trouble areas and avoid pinpointing sites of growing tension and possible trouble in a city. Our duty is to report the story when it develops. We should no more predict violence than we would predict a bank run.
- Regard with suspicion any interviewing of participants during riots. It is questionable whether such interviews serve a valid purpose, and they may incite rather than inform. Trained persons, including police, officials, and articulate onlookers may offer useful facts.

Source: Adapted from CBS' production standards and NBC's guidelines, in Edwin Diamond's *Sign Off: The Last Days of Television* (Cambridge, MA: MIT Press, 1982), p. 57. Copyright © 1982, MIT Press.

when watching newscasts on TV. (Older students may want to research and report on TV codes of news coverage dating from the 1960s.)

CONCLUSION

A newscast is not a simple and objective report of the day's events. It is subject to all kinds of pressures—from journalistic integrity and time restrictions to the number of viewers the program will attract and hold. It is also subject to what newscasters choose to show; reporters covering a political convention might be more interested in showing the people wearing elephant hats than delegates weeping for joy. Newscasters covering a demonstration could have protestors framed by the TV screen in such a way that viewers will think there were large numbers of protestors outside the frame as well when, in fact, there weren't.

By taking a more critical look at the way news and politics are handled on TV, students can gain a better understanding of the issues surrounding broadcast news, and how what audiences see and hear is the result of a variety of factors.

NOTES

1. Leonard Sellers, "How Television Sells the News," *San Francisco* Magazine, (Nov. 1981): 74.

2. Edwin Diamond, *Sign Off: The Last Days of Television* (Cambridge, MA: The Massachusetts Institute of Technology, 1982), p. 56.

3. George C. Conklin, "News and Values," in Logan, *Television Awareness Training: The Viewer's Guide for Family and Community* (New York: Media Action Research Center, 1979), p. 97.

4. Ibid., p. 98.

5. Jonathan Friendly, "Do TV's Lights Illuminate Justice?" *The New York Times,* 29 April, 1984.

6. Ibid.

7. Diamond, *Sign-Off,* p. 179.

8. Ibid., p. 184.

9. David Blomquist, *Elections and the Mass Media* (Washington, DC: the American Political Science Association, 1981), p. 4.

10. "Making the News: A PTST Curriculum Project," prepared by Prime Time School Television, 1979. Supplement to *Media and Methods,* Oct. 1979.

11. Leonard Sellers, "How Television Sells the News," pp. 66–75.

Afterword

Between 1950 and 1980 TV programming was limited by the scarcity of channels on the VHF dial. Now, however, developments in both cable and satellite technology have provided for the transmission of hundreds of channels to viewers. Services such as viewdata and teletext make it possible to receive information from all over the world, and fiber optics and multichannel microwave systems can interconnect home TV sets with computer terminals. All this plus subscription TV, inexpensive VCRs and ITV courses are giving viewers a greater variety of programs and information than ever before.

Youngsters will no doubt be spending more time in front of TV screens as TV and computers become increasingly tied to both school and recreational activities. More TV viewing, however, means less opportunity for learning through direct experience and personal contact with others. It will reduce even further the time children spend with parents and teachers talking about feelings and ways of dealing with problems, causing youngsters to continue to use TV heroes and one dimensional people as role models. They will continue to see unrealistic lifestyles and televised violence and will continue to be told that all their problems can be solved with products such as deodorant or cosmetics.

One way to counteract these negative aspects of TV viewing is to help children heighten their TV literacy. By providing opportunities for discussion children can be encouraged to examine all sides of the many issues they see presented on TV. By helping children to make their own decisions about TV and by preparing them to use TV more wisely it can become a more positive force in their adult lives.

Appendix A: Programs that Work

Video is one of the finest educational tools that children can relate to. It provides a method for recording all aspects of the human experience—from celebrations to tragedies; education to entertainment—while involving its viewers in all aspects of the learning process. Video enables students to examine the world they live in, gather and process information and recognize their own abilities to create change. Many teachers and administrators have recognized the value of using video with students. Several school programs that involve television viewing and production are highlighted below.

• As part of a project designed to promote the humanities, called "Beyond Technology," 13 Marin County, CA, high school students videotaped interviews of such notables as filmmaker Francis Ford Coppola, the late Frank Oppenheimer (founder of the Exploratorium in San Francisco), the president of a local university, an Olympic gold medalist, and poets Lawrence Ferlinghetti and Rosalie Moor.

• In Natchez, MS, a group of vocational school students took a training course covering the utilization and care of a single-camera video system. At the end of the course, students were divided into groups by their respective trade areas. They worked with their instructors and a media specialist to produce several lessons videotaped on location in the school shops (e.g., one production explained the principles of geometric construction as they apply to drafting classes). The video lessons were made available for use by other schools and the community.

• Teachers at the Perry L. Drew School in East Windsor, NJ, discovered a public access clause in the community's cable TV franchise and decided to produce children's programs. Cable TV personnel helped a unit leader, librarian and two first grade teachers produce a series of half-hour segments of stories, songs and activities designed not only to interest children but to complement the school curriculum. Teachers were able to follow up on the programs in their classrooms, and books that were highlighted in the programs were made available in the school library.

• In Mount Vernon, NY, TV scripts are used as the basis of a remedial reading program for junior high school students. Vocabulary words taken from the script are pronounced, defined and used in sentences. Students are asked to determine whether or not a word is used correctly then a segment of the program containing the word (or term) is shown. Students are taped reading the script aloud. Students can also prepare their own video ads for books they read on their own.

Although youngsters who don't read at their current grade level may be reluctant to read aloud, most students in this program enjoy reading the scripts and are at ease in front of the camera. The program is economical (allowing teachers to work with four times as many students than before), and students have shown average reading gains of 2.3 years.

• Ninth through twelfth graders enrolled in the Herricks High School Student Television Arts Company (Long Island, NY) specialize in art, dance, drama, music and voice, as well as video. After students have mastered the use of studio equipment they learn about writing and script development. Students research and dramatize scripts, compose and perform original music, design costumes and sets, choreograph and perform dances, and tape and edit all productions. (These productions may be shown to classes in the elementary and middle schools, as well as in the high school and on cable TV.) Students also design logos and brochures for programs and handle other aspects of public relations.

The students from Herricks High School can also tape on location. For example, when visiting a nearby estate, groups of students representing each area of the arts were given particular locations on the estate to use as a backdrops for three minute mini-productions.

Students from the Company are also given opportunities to observe and meet with professionals. On one occasion, a set designer for a popular TV entertainment program visited the high school and showed students how a model for a basic set used on the program could be modified to accommodate various skits. Several students were subsequently invited to a live taping of the show to observe camera placement and movement.

• For a final project in the Mass Media/Creative Writing Workshop at St. Mary's High School in Rutherford, NJ, students were asked to produce TV shows. The class was divided into three groups. Each group was asked to produce a TV show that would elicit specific emotions. To fully complete the project, students had to include two commercials directed at a target audience, write radio spots announcing the show's premiere and prepare promotional ads for newspapers and magazines. One group that was working on a military recruitment program targeted a teenage/early

20s audience. The group chose to advertise in men's, women's and sports magazines and on rock and country radio stations. It advertised beer, sneakers and sporting events during the show. To elicit the prescribed emotions, the show depicted the difficulties young adults have adjusting and showed the pride and feeling of accomplishment they could find in the military.

• The Dufief Elementary School (Montgomery County, MD) expanded the use of its closed circuit TV system by having third through sixth graders produce daily 10-minute news shows. In addition to editorials on subjects such as energy conservation, interviews and reports on field trips to zoos and wildlife centers, the newscast included a daily weather report. To prepare the weather report, a student checked the school's weather station (for the temperature, wind direction, humidity level and barometric pressure), the daily newspaper, early moring TV reports and local telephone company weather reports. The student reporter marked a map indicating temperatures and approaching fronts that might affect the local weather, and also mentioned constellations and other stellar objects that would be visible in the night sky.

• The Arlington Schools Telecommunications Center (Arlington, VA) is equipped with state-of-the-art color video equipment. It provides services for all high school students in the county interested in pursuing careers in the field of telecommunications and provides classes in video production for students and teachers. The Center also produces instructional and enrichment programs for the educational community.

• Three school districts in Michigan used a television drama, *Family Reunion* (a production that focused on a retired teacher's fight to save her New England homestead by organizing a family reunion to reacquaint relatives with their heritage) to explore family relationships with children in the early grades and family histories with those in the upper grades. The Minneapolis Institute of Arts and Minnesota PTA invited families to view the same program and participate in related museum tours.

Family Reunion and other TV programs have been used nationwide to trace family roots in local museums, to discuss costumes and unfamiliar objects in museums, to explore communication through words and visual arts, and to understand the values museums preserve.

• The Mamaroneck, NY, school system has had an extensive media program for many years. In the kindergarten and first grades students are introduced to records, filmstrips, tapes of children's classics, films and a few videotapes. Second graders develop concepts about light and dark, and children in the middle grades learn ways to tell stories with pictures. These students also make pinhole cameras, develop film and create storyboards. Fifth graders begin to use a TV studio in one of the schools and become active producers, scriptwriters and interviewers. Sixth graders manage all aspects of three-camera video production, and high school students may elect to participate in the Performing Arts Curriculum Education program which centers on experiences with TV production and the arts.

• School District No. 6, which encompasses 15 schools in upper Manhattan, was the first school district in New York City to feed programs directly into a local cable TV system. It now has the most extensive video program in the city. Most video production takes place in the middle schools from grades 5 to 9; some high school students who were involved at these levels return later as video interns.

Two groups started producing tapes in 1971 when the district received federal funds for the purchase of video equipment. "The United Children's Press," began operating after school from a small district studio. It involved students and teachers in the production of programs modeled after broadcast news shows. Another group, "School Rap" produced news programs that dealt with nontraditional subjects such as career education, bilingual programming and conflict resolution. Students in both of these groups conducted all the research and made all the preparations necessary for producing the news. Their tapes were subsequently shown on cable channels throughout New York.

During the mid-1970s students operated out of several studios. The following programs were produced by students during this period:

Celebration—A series that featured puppet shows, musicals and bilingual dramatizations.

District 6 Speaks—A weekly cable series that focused on a variety of topics such as museums, Pan American Day, and "Unwitnessed News" (a parody of a network TV station's local newscasts); interviews with the mayor, other political figures, artists, dancers and people in the community; and programs produced by teachers for teachers (e.g., a tape on the work of a physical education instructor who had done revolutionary work in the area of movement with handicapped children).

Salute to Viking—An award-winning program in which children interviewed, via satellite, the three leading NASA scientists who had designed the Viking spacecraft.

Watt Went Wrong—A program that dealt with the energy crisis and possible solutions.

Best Bets—Three shows sponsored by the local PBS affiliate that focused on the danger of hazardous materials being shipped over the George Washington Bridge and through the Washington Heights area of Manhattan.

Currently, over 100 gifted/talented students from District 6 are participating in a "Saturday Academy" program. Other students throughout the district continue to document festivals, performances and other activities that take place in the schools. These students also produce tapes on themes such as child abuse, nuclear proliferation, constitutional rights, citizenship and voting. One recent project on nutrition included an interview with a science reporter for *The New York Times*. Another project in cooperation with the Lincoln Center Institute resulted in the creation of an operetta on the subject of "no smoking." The operetta was written and produced entirely by students.

Additional projects (either planned or in operation) include an oral history project with a senior citizens center, a collaboration on broadcasts with Superstation WTBS (a satellite cable TV network with over 35 million viewers), use of a video-mobile to serve the community, exhibit of student-produced tapes in local stores, the airing of public service announcements on PBS and cable TV (spots have already appeared on several stations including Music Television), and establishment of a central TV studio in the district.

Appendix B: Jobs in Television

Students often express interest in performing on television. They are usually not aware of what such a job would involve, however, and are unfamiliar with the many career options that exist behind the scenes. By exploring a variety of TV-related jobs, students may not only become more aware of the many opportunities available in areas such as TV production, sales and broadcasting, but they may also get a better picture of how the industry is organized and how a large number of people contribute to the final product.

Job opportunities in all areas of television are expected to increase. In addition to positions within the standard broadcast TV industry, there are also opportunities within the thousands of cable TV systems operating in the U.S. Industries, corporations, manufacturers, hospitals, insurance companies, government agencies, educational facilities, military units, banks, retail stores, utilities, and energy and transportation concerns have all been using TV for a variety of purposes. These include instruction, motivational training, surveillance, teleconferencing, public relations, and the creation of in-house news and feature programs.

Invite a professional from a local station, perhaps one who works in a field in which students have expressed interest, to talk with your class about his or her job. Have students prepare general questions such as those listed below:

- What opportunities exist in the field?
- How would you describe a typical day?
- Do you work with other people? Who do you report to?
- Do you use special equipment?

- How did you prepare for this job? What special training or experience did you find helpful? What educational requirements and skills were necessary?
- How did you break into the field?
- Were any personal interests or hobbies influential in your career decision?
- Do you enjoy your work?

Students can also prepare questions appropriate for specific fields. For example, they might ask a writer the following questions:

- Where do you get ideas for a story line?
- Do you work alone or with others?
- Do you follow any guidelines?
- How long does it usually take to write a script? How many times might a script need to be revised? Do you ever use a storyboard? Who has final approval over the script?
- Do you write for only one type of program? Is writing for one particular type of program easier than writing for another?
- What does a shooting script look like? Are there scripts for talk programs and game shows? Do scripts for news and sports broadcasts, promotions, advertisements, documentaries, variety and children's programs all look the same?
- What rights do you have to express opinions, popular or otherwise? If you take a position on a controversial issue, do you have to incorporate opposing views into the script? If you incorporate opposing views, does it weaken the script and its impact?

Students might ask performers questions such as what time they have to get up for work; how long it takes to tape a program or commercial; what parts they like to play; or what the statistics are concerning the employment of performers on TV.

A station manager might discuss what it takes to create a station's profile or image. A news director might talk about the news, what should be the news and how he or she selects, prioritizes and assigns news stories. A cameraperson might discuss how working with a TV camera differs from using a motion picture camera.

A special effects person could talk about animation techniques, and other professionals could discuss and/or demonstrate areas such as makeup, lighting, costumes, set design and TV criticism.

TV JOBS

The following is a selection of job opportunities within the TV industry and their descriptions.

Programming/Production*

Producer, overall administrator responsible for the quality and content of productions. Supervises the crew and director (and sometimes writers and artists); organizes meetings and schedules; works with sales representatives and public relations personnel; and reads and revises scripts. In a large studio, the executive producer is in charge of one or more TV series, while the producer is in charge of individual productions. Additional responsibilities of the producer in a small studio might include writing, directing, selection of topics for talk programs, as well as the securing of talent and the briefing of guests.

Director, provides a unified view for programs, ensures that one scene flows smoothly into another; coordinates the efforts of talent and technicians; determines the positions of cameras and talent and indicates them on a floor plan; works with the producer, scriptwriter, artist, assistant director, talent, camera operators and stage manager; chooses music and sound effects and prepares a list of tapes and records for the sound technician; prepares a list of shots for the camera operators; controls color, light and picture quality and cues technicians and camera operators from the control room; helps edit the videotape.

Assistant Director or **Continuity Person,** helps the director by noting everything that goes on in each shot on the set and on location. Writes a narrative report based on these notes which is used by the director and videotape editor.

Writer, creates scripts usually in a standard format that describe how a program will look and sound.

Researcher, supplies facts for a newscast, documentary, docudrama or story (especially one requiring an authentic setting).

Artist, creates all the visuals for a production: sets, drawings, animation, storyboards, title cards, captions and signs. May sketch courtroom scenes and create graphics such as maps and symbols. Additional responsibilities can include photography research (for authenticity), set building, prop construction and preparation of graphics for in-house publications.

Talent, includes actors, actresses, singers, dancers, musicians, and hosts and guests on talk programs.

Camera Operator, composes the picture, adjusts camera angles; works from director's shot list; and checks that equipment is operating properly. Works closely with the director to achieve his or her objectives. Sometimes has to operate and move heavy equipment.

---

*Many small stations do not have all of these classifications and divide the work differently. Larger stations may have additional job classifications and support services.

Lighting Director, provides effective lighting by studying the script and working with the director to determine lighting needs.

Floor Manager, communicates (through hand signals) the director's orders to crew and performers during rehearsals, live broadcasts and taped sessions. Supervises stagehands and oversees the construction and placement of sets; checks settings, microphones, lights, props and graphics.

Traffic Manager, ensures that program schedules are accurate and that programs and commercials appear at the right time by logging them in the proper order each day; orders audio cartridges, films and slides, and checks their quality. Notes dated or offensive materials, verifies the accuracy of times recorded on each tape cartridge; obtains tapes and backup programs to fill unused air time (e.g., when a live event ends earlier than expected); may maintain the station's tape library where cartridges and videotapes are cataloged and stored.

Technical

Chief Engineer, responsible for all the technical aspects of a broadcast. Oversees the installation, repair and maintenance of video control and videotape operations; arranges for the acquisition of new equipment (with approval of the station manager); and hires and assigns technicians. Additional responsibilities may include setting the station's engineering policy, interpreting broadcast regulations and handling business matters (in a large station, these are the responsibilities of the director of engineering).

Master Control Engineer, ensures that the correct programming material, received from various sources (the studio, network, and remote lines), appears at the right time. Regulates the stations transmitter; takes power readings; is responsible for the overall technical quality of programs.

Switcher Operator, operates the editing device that electronically mixes (dissolves one picture into another); creates special effects; inserts or removes scenes, film clips and slides; switches back and forth between studio and remote locations; ensures smooth transitions; previews programs.

Videocontrol Engineer, controls the picture quality for the station by adjusting the camera control unit.

Videotape Operator, operates the machine used for post-production editing; tapes the shots, film clips and graphics together in the proper order.

Technical Director, responsible for the sound and picture quality of the production; operates the videocontrol board during live broadcasts; chooses the right time to show slides, film clips and tapes; edits videotaped programs.

Audio Engineer, operates the audio console consisting of tape cartridges, magnetic recorders, record turntables and sound mixers; produces sound effects requested by the director; checks and adjusts microphones; maintains audio equipment.

Character Generator Operator, operates the electronic machine that lists the credits; arranges material in order before taping begins; types printed bits of information and stores them in the machine's memory bank.

News Division

News Director, oversees the entire news operation and staff; is responsible for finances and union negotiations; keeps up with laws regulating news reporting; scans wire services for news reports; works with the producer and director of the news program to decide which events are to be reported.

Director, directs cameras, film and videotape projection.

News Producer, selects the news; determines the length and sequence of stories.

Assistant Director or **Production Assistant,** makes certain that all necessary changes have been made and that the correct script has been distributed; arranges for credits to appear; orders visuals and maintains them on file.

Assignment Editor, sends staff and camera crews to various locations.

Writer, prepares the script.

News Reporter, works with (and sometimes directs) film crews on location; may rewrite stories that come over the news wire or report a story on location or from the studio.

Anchor, delivers the news from the studio; pulls together reports from correspondents; provides transitions and creates a sense of order; often researches and writes own scripts.

Sports Director, directs, administers and supervises the sports department; assigns reporters to cover events; may cover and report some events; prepares scripts; narrates telecasts; edits videotapes of sports stories.

Administration

Station Manager, chief executive, responsible for the actions of employees and the success or failure of the station; answers only to the station's owners or corporate board of directors; interprets and carries out rules and regulations issued by the

FCC; oversees records; prepares for FCC inspections; and solves problems in operations. Works with the program director and sales executive to formulate the station's objectives and policies.

Director of Programming or Operations Director, helps set operations policy and develop budgets; coordinates major productions that originate at the station; attempts to develop quality local programs of all types; directs the purchase of programs from outside suppliers and from the networks.

Utilization Specialist, helps teachers, parents and community leaders use TV for educational purposes.

Sales and Promotion

Advertising Director, plans ads and other promotions for TV, radio, and periodicals; prepares materials for sales representatives.

Sales Representative, meets with prospective buyers of TV air time; prepares for meeting these clients by researching products in relation to station's programs and time schedules; identifies available spots; researches the type, size of viewing audience and ratings for each program.

Public Relations Director, responsible for the station's image; generates rapport between the station and community by preparing press releases announcing the stations activities and other news of interest to viewers; arranges for new programs to be reviewed; publicizes and interviews performers; arranges for local talent to appear in the community; helps people who contact the station for information.

Appendix C: Video Games

Some parents have expressed concern about what video games may be doing to their children. Parent-Teacher Associations and neighborhood organizations are concerned that video game arcades are a social menace and home video games along with TV programming replace other activities and add to the number of hours children spend facing a TV screen.

While ads show scenes of families gathered happily around a video game, the family actually has nothing much to talk about except winning the game. Many of the games are violent and war-like, and don't allow time for reflection. Critics have also speculated that the ability to control fantasy worlds in video games could make some children impatient with the often uncontrollable world of real life.

However, despite these concerns, video games can play a positive role in education. They can heighten sensorimotor skills, develop spatial and geometric perception, allow for interaction and control (an aspect important for teenagers), heighten eye-hand coordination and promote orientation toward independent achievement. Video games provide a good introduction to computers and, when designed for specific educational purposes, can have great potential as teaching devices. For example, there have been games on the market that teach health and fitness such as *Plaque Attack* made by ActiVision (where a tube of toothpaste defends a set of eight healthy teeth from an onslaught of junk-food invaders) and *Microsurgeon* by Imagic (where the player guides a "probe" with weapons at its disposal such as ultrasound, antibiotics or aspirin through a patient's circulatory system)—to name just a few educational applications.

Video games share some things in common with conventional games such as randomness and speed. Other aspects—i.e., automatic score keeping, audio effects and certain types of complexity—are only available electronically. Whereas a conventional board game gives a player all the rules, some computer games require players to induce the rules through observation, causing players to exercise their inductive skills. Students who become skillful video games players can also develop proficiency in parallel processing (taking in information from several sources simultaneously), as well as the ability to look at variables one at a time and as they interact with and influence each other. Playing video games can also help students develop the ability to coordinate visual information coming from multiple perspectives.

As teaching aids, video games provide individual feedback and can help teachers to determine how well a child is responding. These games can also be designed so that the player must use previously acquired knowledge. Action can be sped up or new elements introduced to challenge players, and different levels of difficulty can demonstrate a player's progress as well as stimulate interest in the next level.

Appendix D: Off-Air Recording

The Supreme Court ruled in January 1984 that it is legal to use video recorders to tape television programs for personal use. In Sony Corporation of America v. Universal City Studios Inc. the court held that the noncommercial use of videotape recorders in the home does not violate federal copyright laws.

The Court notes that both sides in the case agreed that the primary use of home video recorders was for "time-shifting"—i.e., the recording of a program for later, more convenient viewing. Such private, noncommercial use falls within the "fair-use" exception to the legal right to control the use of copyrighted material, outlined by Congress in the 1976 amendments to the federal copyright laws. The Sony case may in the future be interpreted to allow greater use of videotaped material by schools, but for now the "fair use" guidelines worked out by educators and representatives of the entertainment industry a few years ago should be adhered to.

These guidelines (listed below) allow teachers in nonprofit educational institutions to tape broadcast material that might be useful in the classroom. Central audiovisual departments may also tape material at the individual request of teachers, but not on a blanket basis. A teacher can tape a program at home as can any other citizen, but when the tape is brought to school, the limitations apply.

GUIDELINES FOR OFF-AIR RECORDING OF BROADCAST PROGRAMMING FOR EDUCATIONAL PURPOSES

1. The guidelines were developed to apply only to off-air recording by non-profit educational institutions.

2. A broadcast program may be recorded off-air simultaneously with broadcast transmission (including simultaneous cable retransmission) and retained by a non-profit educational institution for a period not to exceed the first forty-five (45) consecutive calendar days after date of recording. Upon conclusion of such retention period, all off-air recordings must be erased or destroyed immediately. "Broadcast programs" are television programs transmitted by television stations for reception by the general public without charge.

3. Off-air recordings may be used once by individual teachers in the course of relevant teaching activities, and repeated once only when instructional reinforcement is necessary, in classrooms and similar places devoted to instruction within a single building, cluster or campus, as well as in the homes of students receiving formalized home instruction, during the first ten (10) consecutive school days in the forty-five (45) days calendar day retention period. "School days" are school session days—not counting weekends, holidays, vacations, examination periods, or other scheduled interruptions—within the forty-five (45) calendar day retention period.

4. Off-air recordings may be made only at the request of and used by individual teachers, and may not be regularly recorded in anticipation of requests. No broadcast program may be recorded off-air more than once at the request of the same teacher, regardless of the number of times the program may be broadcast.

5. A limited number of copies may be reproduced from each off-air recording to meet the legitimate needs of teachers under these guidelines. Each such additional copy shall be subject to all provisions governing the original recording.

6. After the first ten (10) consecutive school days, off-air recordings may be used up to the end of the forty-five (45) calendar day retention period only for teacher evaluation purposes, i.e., to determine whether or not to include the broadcast program in the teaching curriculum, and may not be used in the recording institution for student exhibition or any other non-evaluation purpose without authorization.

7. Off-air recordings need not be used in their entirety, but the recorded programs may not be altered from their original content. Off-air recordings may not be physically or electronically combined or merged to constitute teaching anthologies or compilations.

8. All copies of off-air recordings must include the copyright notice on the broadcast program as recorded.

9. Educational institutions are expected to establish appropriate control procedures to maintain the integrity of these guidelines.

Reprinted from *Off-Air Videotaping in Education* with permission of the R.R. Bowker Company.

Appendix E: Resources

Students can "talk back" to their TV sets by regulating what they view and by thinking about and discussing how what they watch may be affecting them.

Adults and children who are not satisfied with the programs on a particular TV station, or who feel news reports may not be fair or honest, can complain individually or as a group to the station manager. If a letter is written, carbon copies should be sent to the FCC where they will be filed and possibly used when the station's performance is evaluated. Since operators of local stations may not be the actual owners (who want to make sure that their station's license will be renewed), letters should also be written to the station's owners. Suggest also, that students write to sponsors (and advertisers) of programs that they feel are not produced in the public interest. Networks may not be as responsive to complaints as the local stations since they aren't regulated or licensed by the FCC. However, comments are generally welcomed by stations and sponsors. Group efforts usually receive more attention than those of individuals. The PTA, library associations, YMCA, YWCA, church groups and minority rights organizations such as the National Organization for Women, the Mexican American Council, the Gay Media Task Force and the New York Black Media Coalition—as well as the organizations listed below—are all groups that can help with TV reform. (One organization that has caused significant reform through the use of research, dialogue, publicity and legal action is Action for Children's Television.)

When speaking with station managers, students should understand that while the managers may be just as interested in reform as they are, managers also have a financial interest to protect. Students should be friendly but also wary of "public relations" talk. It is also important that, if students complain, they add credibility to their case by being able to name people and organizations that support their efforts. Students should clarify their concerns and questions and offer specific suggestions concerning what they would like to have done. If students are dissatisfied with the station's response, at the time of a station's license renewal a citizen "Petition to Deny Renewal" can be filed with the FCC (this action requires the services of an attorney).

COMMERCIAL AND PUBLIC BROADCASTING NETWORKS

American Broadcasting Comanies, Inc.
1330 Ave. of the Americas
New York, NY 10019

The Division of Community Relations provides background materials for *ABC Afterschool* and *Weekend Specials*.

Columbia Broadcasting System
51 West 52nd St.
New York, NY 10019

The CBS Television Reading Program provides scripts and viewers' guides through local affiliates for special CBS programs.

National Broadcasting Company
30 Rockefeller Plaza
New York, NY 10020

Viewers' guides are available for special NBC presentations. NBC also sponsors the Scholastic Writing Awards for students in grades 7 through 12.

Public Broadcasting Service
475 L'Enfant Plaza, SW
Washington, DC 20024

Descriptions of forthcoming programs and other materials are available.

ORGANIZATIONS AND PROGRAMMING SERVICES

Action for Children's Television
46 Austin St.
Newtonville, MA 02160

National organization working to upgrade the quality of children's television. Publishes a magazine and a variety of other books and pamphlets.

Agency for Instructional Technology
Box A
Bloomington, IN 47401

Resources and programming concerning the educational uses of television.

Children's Advertising Review Unit
Council of Better Business Bureaus, Inc.
845 Third Ave.
New York, NY 10022

Prepares and publishes guidelines for advertisers of products directed toward children.

Citizens Action for Better Television
1629 Locust St.
Philadelphia, PA 19103

Helps viewers communicate with the industry through the use of viewers cards sent to networks and sponsors.

Cultural Information Service
P.O. Box 786
Madison Square Station
New York, NY 10159

Publishes a magazine and a large number of television viewing guides.

Federal Communications Commission
1919 M St., NW
Washington, DC 20554

Organization that regulates interstate and foreign communications by radio, television, wire and cable.

Kidsnet
1201 16th St., NW
Suite 607-E
Washington, DC 20036

Computerized clearinghouse that includes information on children's television and radio programs.

Media Action Research Center
475 Riverside Dr.
New York, NY 10027

Publishes critical viewing materials and sponsors television awareness training workshops.

National Council for Children and Television
20 Nassau St.
Princeton, NJ 08540

Provides a forum for issues concerning children and television through its publication, *Television and Families.*

National PTA TV Action Center
700 N. Rush St.
Chicago, IL 60611-2571

Publishes pamphlets and news releases designed to improve television literacy from early childhood through adulthood.

National Telemedia Council
120 E. Wilson St.
Madison, WI 53703

Publishes a newsletter and a wide variety of other materials. Conducts the annual national Look-Listen Opinion Poll.

Nickelodeon
1133 Ave. of the Americas
New York, NY 10036

Distributes educational materials for children's cable programs.

Parents' Choice Foundation
P.O. Box 185
Waban, MA 02168

Provides reviews of children's media through its publication, *Parents' Choice.*

The Radio-Television Council of Greater Cleveland, Inc.
1219 James A. Rhodes Tower
Cleveland, OH 44115

Maintains a speakers bureau, conducts polls, holds monthly meetings and distributes other materials. Also sponsors local awards.

Teachers Guides to Television
699 Madison Ave.
New York, NY 10021

Publishes program guides and schedules. Helped develop the Parent Participation TV Workshop project which encourages children, parents, teachers and other interested people to organize and participate in discussion groups.

Yale University Family TV Research/Consultation Center
Box 11A Yale Station
New Haven, CT 06520

Publishes a variety of books and articles concerning research conducted by the Center.

Bibliography

BOOKS

Aaron, Shirley L. and Scales, Pat R., eds. *School Library Media Annual, 1983.* Volume 1. Littleton, CO: Libraries Unlimited, Inc., 1983.

Barcus, F. Earle. *Images of Life on Children's Television: Sex Roles, Minorities, and Families.* New York: Praeger, 1983.

Blomquist, David. *Elections and the Mass Media.* Washington, DC: American Political Science Association, 1981.

Burns, Marilyn. *I Am Not a Short Adult! Getting Good at Being a Kid.* Boston: Little, Brown and Co., 1977.

Cater, Douglas, ed. *Television as a Social Force: New Approaches to TV Criticism.* New York: Praeger, 1975.

Charren, Peggy and Sandler, Martin W. *Changing Channels: Living (Sensibly) with Television.* Reading, MA: Addison-Wesley, 1983.

Charren, Peggy and Alperowicz, Cynthia. *Editors' Choice: A Look at Books for Children's TV.* Newtonville, MA: Action for Children's Television, 1982.

Cheney, Glenn Alan. *Television in American Society.* New York: Franklin Watts, 1983.

Cherry, Colin. *World Communications: Threat or Promise.* New York: Wiley-Interscience, 1978.

Cole, Barry, ed. *Television Today: A Close-Up View.* Oxford: Oxford University Press, 1981.

Cross, Donna Woolfolk. *Media-Speak: How Television Makes Up Your Mind.* New York: Mentor/New American Library, 1983.

Diamond, Edwin. *Sign Off: The Last Days of Television.* Cambridge: The Massachusetts Institute of Technology, 1982.

Doerken, Maurine. *Classroom Combat: Teaching and Television.* Englewood Cliffs, NJ: Educational Technology Publications, 1983.

Fang, I.E. *Television News.* Revised edition. New York: Hastings House, 1972.

Graber, Doris A. *Mass Media and American Politics.* Washington, DC: Congressional Quarterly Press, 1980.

Greenfield, Patricia Marks. *Mind and Media: The Effects of Television, Video Games, and Computers.* Cambridge: Harvard University Press, 1984.

Hays, Kim, ed. *TV, Science, and Kids: Teaching Our Children to Question.* Reading, MA: Addison-Wesley, 1984.

Hollingsworth, T.R. *Tune In to a Television Career.* New York: Julian Messner, 1984.

Johnson, Nicholas. *How to Talk Back to Your Television Set.* New York: Bantam, 1970.

Kavanaugh, Dorriet, ed. *Listen to Us! The Children's Express Report.* New York: Workman, 1978.

Kelley, Michael R. *A Parents' Guide to Television: Making the Most of It.* New York: John Wiley and Sons, 1983.

Lee, Barbara and Rudman, Masha Kabakow. *Mind Over Media: New Ways to Improve Your Child's Reading and Writing Skills.* New York: Seaview Books, 1982.

Logan, Ben, ed. *Television Awareness Training: The Viewer's Guide for Family and Community.* New York: Media Action Research Center, 1979.

Moody, Kate. *Growing Up On Television: A Report to Parents.* New York: McGraw-Hill, 1980.

Pillon, Nancy Bach. *Reaching Young People Through Media.* Littleton, CO: Libraries Unlimited, Inc., 1983.

Potter, Rosemary Lee. *New Season: The Positive Use of Commercial Television with Children.* Columbus, OH: Charles E. Merrill, 1976.

Renowden, Gareth. *Video: The Inside Story.* New York: Gloucester Press, 1983.

Schwarz, Meg, ed. *TV and Teens: Experts Look at the Issues.* Reading, MA: Addison-Wesley, 1982.

Singer, Dorothy G.; Singer, Jerome L.; and Zuckerman, Diana M. *Teaching Television: How to Use TV to Your Child's Advantage.* New York: The Dial Press, 1981.

——— . *Getting the Most Out of TV.* Santa Monica: Goodyear, 1981.

Sinofsky, Esther R. *Off-Air Videotaping in Education: Copyright Issues, Decisions, Implications.* New York: R.R. Bowker, 1984.

Taylor, Paula. *Kid's Whole Future Catalog.* New York: Random House, 1982.

Television Literacy: Critical Televison Viewing Skills. Boston: Dendron Press, 1981.

Wicklein, John. *Electronic Nigthmare: The New Communications and Freedom.* New York: Viking, 1981.

Winn, Marie. *The Plug-In Drug: Television, Children, and the Family.* Revised edition. New York: Penguin Books, 1985.

PERIODICALS, REPORTS, PAMPHLETS AND TEACHER'S GUIDES

Abelman, Robert. "Learning to Learn TV Cues and TVQs." *Television and Children* 7 (Summer/Fall 1984): 13–17.

Alperowicz, Cynthia. "Video Games: What's the Score?" *Re:Act* 12, pp. 10–11.

Burns, John. "Whither Children's Television?" *Telemedium* (March-June 1984): 1–2.

Cable and Children: An ACT Handbook. Newtonville, MA: Action for Children's Television, 1981.

The Chronicle of Higher Education, 17 October 1984.

——— , 13 March 1985.

Comstock, George. "Education and Television: The Persistent Challenge." *Television and Children* 5 (Summer 1982): 9–13.

———. "Television's Four Highly Attracted Audiences." *New York Univeristy Education Quarterly* 9 (Winter 1978): 23–28.

Critical TV Viewing Skills Training Manual. Austin: Southwest Educational Development Laboratory, 1979.

Dale, Donna. "Television Reporting: Student Style." *Science and Children* (February 1981). (Reprint.)

DeMaio, Ronald. "The Student Television Arts Company." *Design for Arts in Education* (Jan./Feb. 1983): 27–31.

Education Week (21 Dec. 1983).

———. (25 Jan. 1984).

Emmens, Carol A. "Docudramas—Revised History?" *Previews* (May 1980): 2–4.

Family Learning, May/June 1984, "The Family Learning Guide."

"Family Problems: How They've Affecting Classrooms Today." *Learning 86* (Jan 1986): 36–37.

Fantel, Hans. "On Location." *Ballet News* (June 1984): 28–29.

Fighting TV Stereotypes: An ACT Handbook. Newtonville, MA: Action for Children's Television, 1983.

Freeman, Debra. "A New Use for Television: Leading Families to Museums." *Teachers' Guides to Television* (Spring 1982). (Reprint.)

Greene, Bob. "Television, the Violent Intruder." *San Francisco Chroncile* (27 Jan. 1985) "This World," p. 5.

Inside Out: A Guide for Teachers. Bloomington, IN: National Instructional Television Center, 1973.

Kahn, Linda Merle. "Evening TV Can Work for You." *Better Broadcasts News* (Feb. 1980): 8.

———. "A Practical Guide to Critical TV Viewing Skills." *Media and Methods* (Oct. 1979): 32.

Kaplan, Don. "Even Networks Have a Silver Lining." *Design for Arts in Education* (Sept./Oct. 1983): 42–43.

——. "The 40,000-Mile Phone Call." *Learning* (Feb. 1984): 95–100.

Krock, Robert. "Big Sell on the Small Screen." *PTA Today* (March 1985): 36–37.

"Making the News: A PTST Curriculum Project." *Media and Methods* (Oct. 1979). (Insert.)

Marc, David. "Understanding Television." *The Atlantic Monthly* (Aug. 1984): 33–44.

Morrisett, Lloyd N. "Television, America's Neglected Teacher." *Television and Children* 7 (Summer/Fall 1984): 39–45.

The New York Times, 21 April 1984.

——, 24 April 1984.

——, 29 April 1984.

——, 16 July 1984.

——, 24 August 1984.

——, 5 May 1985, sec. H., p. 26.

Nielsen Report on Television: 1984. Northbrook, IL: A.C. Nielsen Company, 1984.

The Old Junkman: Teacher's Guide. New York: CBS Television Reading Program, CBS Television Network, 1983.

Paine, Carolyn. "Teachers Who Make the Difference." *Learning* (March 1984): 20.

"Petition for Rulemaking Pertaining to Children's Advertising Detector Signal Before the Federal Communications Commission." Washington, DC 1983. (Mimeographed.)

Riccobono, John A. *School Utilization Study: Availability, Use, and Support of Instructional Media.* Washington, DC: Corporation for Public Broadcasting, 1985.

Rowe, Marieli. "Media Literacy: The New Challenge." *Better Broadcasts News* (March/April 1981): 1, 6.

San Francisco Chronicle, 21 July 1982.

——, 28 October 1983.

——, 12 February 1985.

——, 16 March 1985.

——, 11 September 1985.

San Francisco Examiner, 1 July 1984.

——, 22 July 1984, Sec. A, p. A10.

——, 7 October 1984, "Datebook," pp. 50–51.

——, 30 December 1984, "TV Week," p. 3.

——, 28 July 1985, Sec. D, p. D1.

San Jose Mercury News, 26 June 1984.

——, 28 June 1984.

——, 29 June 1984.

——, 28 August 1984.

Sellers, Leonard. "How Television Sells the News." *San Francisco* (November 1981): 66–75.

Singer, Dorothy and Kelly, Helen Bryman. *Parents, Children and TV: A Guide to Using TV Wisely* (Columbus, OH: Highlights for Children, 1984).

Singer, Dorothy G. "Family Ties: Sex at Sixteen?" *Television and Children* 7 (Spring 1984): 27–28.

Socha, A. Victoria. "In Conversation with Gary David Goldberg." *Television and Children* 7 (Spring 1984): 19–25.

Someday You'll Find Her, Charlie Brown! Teacher's Guide. New York: CBS Television Reading Program, CBS Television Network, 1983.

Standby. . .Lights! Camera! Action! Chicago: Prime Time School Television, 1983.

Sturken, Marita. "Hey, Kids, Let's Put on A Show. . ."

Sturken, Marita. "Hey, Kids, Let's Put on A Show. . ." *Home Video* (Oct. 1980): 36–37.

——. "Gene Youngblood Forecasts the Communications Revolution." *Sightlines* (Summer 1983): 13, 16.

Take a Lesson From TV: A PTST Elementary Curriculum Project. Chicago: Prime Time School Television, 1980.

The Television Picture. New York: CBS Television Network, 1981.

Ulster County Gazette, 25 February 1982.

U.S. News and World Report, February 18, 1985, p. 65.

Wall Street Journal, 22 April 1985.

Index

About the Author

Don Kaplan has more than 15 years' experience in instructional design for elementary, graduate, adult and special education settings. Currently a contributing editor at *Instructor* magazine, he is a former staff writer for *Learning* magazine, has taught at the Bank Street College of Education, New School for Social Research, University of Nebraska-Lincoln and other colleges, and at various elementary and senior high schools.

Mr. Kaplan is author of *Video in the Classroom* (Knowledge Industry Publications, Inc.) and *See With Your Ears: The Creative Music Book* (Lexikos Press), and a contributor to *Doing the Media* (McGraw-Hill). He has written over 85 articles for magazines including *Media and Methods, Music Educators Journal, Film Library Quarterly* and *Teacher,* and has written a column on video education for *Design for Arts in Education.* He is currently working on a new book, *Children and Media* (Instructor Books), which will be published shortly.